The Life and Adventures of Harvey Teasdale, Converted Clown and Man Monkey

Edited with an introduction and notes by
Rosie Whitcombe, Dawn Hadley, and Vicky Crewe

Victorian Secrets 2018

Published by

Victorian Secrets Limited
32 Hanover Terrace
Brighton BN2 9SN

www.victoriansecrets.co.uk

The Life and Adventures of Harvey Teasdale, Converted Clown and Man Monkey

First published in 1867

This Victorian Secrets edition 2018

Introduction and notes © 2018 by Rosie Whitcombe, Dawn Hadley, and Vicky Crewe
This edition © 2018 by Victorian Secrets

Cover credit iStockPhoto.com/ilbusca

Composition and design by Catherine Pope & Tanya Izzard

A catalogue record for this book is available from the British Library.

ISBN 978-1-906469-63-4

CONTENTS

Introduction   5

Timeline   14

A Note on the Text   16

Acknowledgements   16

About the Editors   16

The Life and Adventures of Harvey Teasdale, The Converted   19
Clown and Man Monkey, with his Remarkable Conversion
in Wakefield Prison

Appendix: Transcripts of Newspaper Articles   95

INTRODUCTION

Harvey Teasdale, Sheffield's 'converted clown and man monkey', was born in Sheffield Park in 1817. Encouraged to follow in his father's footsteps, Teasdale was destined to enter the cutlery trade; from a young age, however, he became enamoured by the allure of the stage. In his youth he began working as a character actor before developing his routine as clown and comedian, performing in numerous pantomimes and harlequinades. Once established in the theatre profession, Teasdale developed the performance that would cement his reputation: the 'man monkey'. A daring display of leaps and tricks, Teasdale's 'man monkey' performance captivated Victorian Sheffield, his success prompting his bravado: 'mine was the best representation of the monkey tribe that ever appeared on the stage'. *The Life and Adventures of Harvey Teasdale* is an autobiographical narrative of a working-class performer, published in the 1860s, several decades before Teasdale's death. It provides a retrospective account of his colourful childhood, the highs and lows of his theatrical career, and his incarceration in Wakefield Prison for attempted murder. *Life and Adventures,* Teasdale claims, was written to promote his subsequent conversion to Methodism and his efforts to rid himself of his 'monkey' alter ego. Published in the wake of his conversion, this confessional text warns its readers about the dangers of alcoholism, ignorance towards religion, and the sins of the stage: 'I pray you shun it, dear reader', Teasdale interjects. Yet it becomes clear through Teasdale's anecdotes and recollections that, despite his best efforts, he remains invested in his performing past.

Structure and Content

The first edition of *Life and Adventures* appears to have been published in 1867. The transcription used in this edition of the text is taken from the twentieth edition, published in 1881, by which time (according to the book's frontispiece) it had sold over 40,000 copies. Bearing in mind Teasdale's penchant for self-promotion, we should perhaps take this number with a pinch of salt. In part, Teasdale used *Life and Adventures* to promote his new career as a public speaker, preaching against the sins of his preconversion life: the 1881 edition includes an address at which Teasdale can be reached to arrange talks.

The information provided by Teasdale in *Life and Adventures* is often sketchy and difficult to verify. For example, he omits dates for many of the events he recounts. In this annotated edition the dates have been identified through extensive research into historical records. We have also drawn on the late Dr Kathleen Barker's largely unpublished work on theatre playbills and papers.[1] Despite the shortcomings of the text, in his autobiography Teasdale presents a uniquely entertaining and informative working-class voice, representing a section of society often overlooked by scholars. Teasdale died in 1904, his life bookending the Victorian period. His autobiography provides rare insight into the vast industrial and social developments that punctuated this era of great change. Working-class Victorian life writing is typically examined as a collective, and consequently individual voices are often silenced, appearing to the historian 'only in the monochromatic glare of a passing riot'.[2] Countering this tradition, Teasdale demands centre stage with his determined writing style and dramatic means of expression.

Life and Adventures can be positioned within the canon of the confessional narrative, a genre that typically requires a revelation of something private. However, these generic expectations cannot be taken as a guarantee of truth. From retrospective self-criticism to reformation of character, Teasdale incorporates a conversion narrative into his confession. The text is divided into two sections: 'The Dark Side', in which Teasdale recounts and rebukes his sinful past; and 'The Light Side', a much shorter section that details the trials and successes of his post-conversion self. 'I was serving Satan and he was paying me my wages': Teasdale repeats this maxim throughout, using it to plot the admonishment that forms the backbone of his autobiography. Yet these pious entreaties are hasty afterthoughts, often tagged on to lengthy retellings of daring adventures. It becomes clear that Teasdale takes more pleasure in regaling his reader with his story than using it to promote religious conversion. Whether he is the 'man-monkey', the messianic man of the people, or the criminal

---

1   Housed in the Kathleen Barker Archive at the University of Bristol's Theatre Collection.

2   David Vincent, *Bread, Knowledge, Freedom: A Study of Nineteenth-Century Working Class Autobiography* (London: Europa, 1981), p. 6.

who imagines himself a wax-work felon in Madame Tussaud's gallery, Teasdale strives, within *Life and Adventures*, for lasting fame.

Early Life

Teasdale recounts numerous anecdotes from his youth to demonstrate how swiftly he 'crept into mischief'. His capering, boasting, stealing, swearing, fighting, skiving and other disruptive behaviours are allegedly presented for the education of his readers, and not for their entertainment. On the first page he expresses regret that he refused to follow his pious mother's example, and as such the accidents that befell him in childhood were, he claims, the devil's punishment for his 'idleness and disobedience to parental commands'. He ends his account of his childhood by lamenting that

> a foundation was laid, so thoroughly blighted and immoral, as to leave
> but little hope for that manly stability and moral integrity of character
> without which it is vain to expect a manhood in any way worthy of
> the name.

Despite Teasdale's moralistic handwringing, he fails to disguise his pride in recounting his youthful exploits; he relives, rather than renounces, his penchant for troublemaking. Revelling in the memory of his classroom capers, Teasdale boasts that his 'influence was so great in the school' his fellow classmates refused to turn him in to their master when he misbehaved, instead heralding him as a schoolyard hero. Teasdale fondly recounts his pugilistic prowess: 'I do not think at that time there was a lad in Sheffield, a stone heavier than myself, could stand any chance with me at fighting, and there scarcely passed a day without their having to test my fighting abilities.' These recollections hint at the performing lifestyle he would soon undertake. Teasdale clearly enjoyed entertaining an admiring audience, recounting the acrobatic skills he would later put to use in his act as 'man monkey'. As a young child he would climb drainpipes and traverse the rooftops of Sheffield, 'running on the slates like a cat'. He would often skip school, preferring instead to cavort in the river fully-dressed to the amusement of local blacksmiths, who would pay him for his tricks. It is when describing his classroom antics that he first refers to his 'monkey skills', amusing his friends 'by leaping through hoops and over chairs like a monkey'. Teasdale's childhood antics anticipate the kind of performing lifestyle he would seek out as a young adult.

Theatrical Career and Attempted Murder

At age thirteen, Teasdale devised a play with some friends. He took
the part of a knight named Hector, and 'certainly, the germ of my new
profession was now sown'. Soon afterwards he visited the theatre for the
first time to see *The London Merchant: The Tragedy of George Barnwell* by
George Lilliol at the Theatre Royal in Sheffield. A story of seduction,
theft, and murder, *The London Merchant* was 'supposed to point out the
evil of sin, to convey a good moral, and to be of great benefit to the
rising youth'. For Teasdale, it only stoked his acting ambitions, and soon
after he established his own Juvenile Amateur Society. This became the
Amateur Theatrical Society, and the troupe began putting on weekly
performances at the Black Beer Brewery pub in Sheffield, favouring
melodramas based on tales of real-life murders and capital punishment.
The amateurish nature of these early performances is best explained
in Teasdale's recollection of *Raymond and Agnes, or the Bleeding Nun*.
The troupe found themselves without an actress to play the Bleeding
Nun's ghost, so Teasdale's fiancée, Sarah, was persuaded to take the part.
However, being 'a stout buxom girl, with cheeks red as the rising sun',
some work was needed to prepare her for the role:

> We dressed her in white (of course without crinoline), together with an
> awful amount of whitening, to hide the roses from her cheeks. The time
> came at length for her to appear, and, alas! as quickly to disappear. Her
> entrance on the scene, that was to have produced universal quaking
> and the rising of the hair like 'quills upon the fretful porcupine', was
> hailed with roars of laughter, and the cry, 'Oh what a fat ghost!'

Sarah's embarrassed retreat from the stage brought an early end to the
show. The audience demanded their money back, but the troupe refused,
and so were forced to make a speedy exit. Similar calamities followed:
fireworks were accidentally ignited during *Don Juan*, the actors were
attacked on stage by drunken 'roughs', and the scenery came crashing
down on the audience during a performance of *The Sea, The Sea, or the
Ocean Child*. Unsurprisingly, the troupe frequently moved premises,
taking rooms at numerous pubs, unable to remain in one place for very
long.

In the 1830s and 40s, Teasdale performed with travelling theatre companies and managed theatrical venues. It was during this period that he recounts one particular performance which 'brought me out more fully in that new character as man monkey, for which I have, since that time, been mainly distinguished'. Another show brought him to Sheffield's Adelphi Theatre during which he 'hit upon the very novel expedient to draw a full house, and it succeeded admirably. I advertised, in flaming placards, that I would sail down the river in a washing-tub drawn by ducks'. We get a glimpse into Teasdale's estimation of his own reputation when he claims a crowd of 70,000 turned out to see him sail down the river, with so many people standing on one wall that it collapsed, sending people tumbling into the water. No lives were lost, Teasdale claims, and his 'stout heart' allowed him to continue the stunt amid the tumult. That night the Adelphi was full and Teasdale's proceedings from his benefit – a supplementary performance after which the actor kept all or most of the profit – were substantial.

Shortly after these events, Teasdale took to the stage as 'man monkey', and his descriptions reveal just how thrilling his performance must have been for an early Victorian audience: 'it was announced that the man monkey would make the daring and unparalleled leap from the gallery to the stage! ... I need hardly say it was a splendid and great financial success'. When performing in Darlington (Co. Durham), his act was considered so convincing that inhabitants placed bets on whether he was, in fact, a real monkey. At Carlisle (Cumbria) in early 1842, 'immense crowds came to witness the exploits of the man monkey, whose tremendous leaps from the gallery to pit or stage seemed to inspire the silly crowds with a kind of monkey mania'. A short-lived experiment with a crocodile act in Hull went down well with the audience, Teasdale claims, but 'did not impress me very favourably with its merits; true, it was greatly applauded, but, if it had not succeeded, mine would have been but crocodile tears for its doom'.

By the early 1850s Teasdale's stage reputation was flourishing, but his personal life was starting to unravel. He was drinking heavily and the considerable income from his engagements was squandered on 'that appetite for strong drink, which made me careless of consequences, reckless, and inexperienced in my speculations'. Surprisingly, this chaotic lifestyle does not seem to have hindered the energy and athleticism of

Teasdale's performances: 'it has often astonished even myself how when in a complete state of inebriation, I have gone through my part without a single bungle, taking those fearful leaps without a single mishap, amidst the plaudits of the admiring public'. Teasdale rarely mentions his domestic circumstances. It is likely that he married his fiancée, Sarah (the 'fat ghost'), in the mid-to-late 1830s, as she gave birth to their first daughter Sarah Ann in 1838, and their second, Harriett, in 1842. None of these significant events are, however, mentioned in *Life and Adventures*. He also fails to mention that he was brought before the Sheffield Magistrates in March 1845 for deserting his family to perform with Dick Ryan's travelling company.[3] *Life and Adventures* does not focus on Teasdale's domestic life, until the dramatic events of 1862 unfold.

In chapter six, Teasdale provides a brief and rather sanitised account of the events leading up to his incarceration. He omits details for the sake of 'delicacy', but expresses his growing fear that his wife and daughters had started working as prostitutes. Perhaps unsurprisingly, during this period his wife and daughters left him on multiple occasions, and the family members scattered to different addresses. Teasdale attacks their morality, as well as his own: 'I had surrounded them with influences whose pollution angelic natures alone could withstand. That they should have succumbed was to be expected; I alone was to blame'. The crescendo of this domestic drama came in August 1862, when Teasdale, armed with a blank pistol (there is no mention of the fact that it was blank in *Life and Adventures*) and a razor, broke into the house where his wife was staying, shot at her and inflicted wounds to her face, hands, and neck with the razor, before attempting to cut his own throat. He is vague about the details of this event in his own recollections, but contemporary newspaper reports allow us to fill in many of the gaps (see appendix). We receive the impression of a desperate and unstable man, convinced of his wife's infidelity, angry that she would not return to him, with the intention of scaring her and killing himself.[4] At his trial, Teasdale was lucky to be found guilty of the lesser crime of unlawful wounding rather

---

3   *Sheffield Iris*, 'The Clown in a Different Character', 27th March, 1845.

4   *Sheffield & Rotherham Independent*, 'Attempted Murder and Suicide at Sheffield', 5th August, 1862; *Sheffield and Rotherham Independent*, 'The Attempted Murder and Suicide' 6th August, 1862; *Sheffield & Rotherham Independent*, 'The Charge Against Harvey Teasdale', 13th December, 1862.

than attempted murder, arrived at because the pistol was blank and the wounds he inflicted on his wife were superficial and not life-threatening. He was sentenced to two years' hard labour in Wakefield Prison, and it is at this juncture that 'The Dark Side' of his narrative ends. Ever hungry for fame, Teasdale cannot resist taking an aside to contemplate what his reputation as a 'celebrity' murderer might have been, had he succeeded in killing his wife:

> Thus ends the dark side of my life, but not my life itself. It might have been closed with the last dying speech and confession of a malefactor, a murderer, with the halter round his neck, a felon's grave within the precincts of the prison, and probably honoured with a niche in Madame Tussaud's dark gallery of celebrated criminals.

Imprisonment and Conversion

During his time in prison, Teasdale claims to have converted from his life of sin in the country's theatrical underbelly. On his release in November 1864, he resolved never to return to the stage or the bottle, and, turning down a sum of £7 to resume his performance, he returned to Sheffield. His love of performing was not entirely spent, however; very quickly Teasdale became a preacher with the Hallelujah Band, which was making a name for itself in Sheffield's temperance halls and chapels hosting rousing conversion rallies. One suspects that the boisterous audience was not much different from his 'man monkey' crowd; at one lively Chesterfield (Derbyshire) meeting he declares 'cries of mercy were heard from all parts of the chapel, and no attempt was made to check these audible cries'.

Teasdale's stage costumes, scripts, and props soon became useful again, when, in January 1865, Teasdale and the Hallelujah Band announced their intention to publicly destroy them in a final exorcism of his monkey alter ego. In front of a rowdy crowd at Sheffield's Temperance Hall, the band destroyed his clown costumes, manuscripts, and – in a dramatic finale – the monkey costume, padded with sawdust to render it more life-like.[5] Teasdale's claim that the items were 'burnt upon the stage' is unsubstantiated by the newspaper reports. During the Temperance Hall event Teasdale was accused of having pulled the same stunt in Leeds; 'I

---

5 *Sheffield & Rotherham Independent*, 'The Man Monkey in a New Character', 24th January, 1865.

have enemies in Leeds', was Teasdale's weak defence.[6]

Contrary to Teasdale's assertions that he had left the iniquity of the stage behind, his new 'act' developed swiftly, to the consternation of several local newspapers. One correspondent accused Teasdale of making money from his sermonising and remarked that 'decency is outraged, religion burlesqued' by the Hallelujah Band events.[7] Irked to discover that he was accused of the 'pious dodge' (in other words, profiting by his preaching), Teasdale took to the road again, this time as a pedlar and travelling preacher. Accompanied by his donkey, Charley, he roamed North Derbyshire and South Yorkshire, before returning to Sheffield and his long-suffering wife. The general attitude towards Teasdale did not appear to soften during his time on the road. Several contemporary newspaper reports were heavily critical, one account threatening that 'the Man Monkey be aware of the fists, cudgels and horse whips',[8] and another that he is 'being hunted out of every corner in which he may happen to hide'.[9]

The autobiography ends with Teasdale returning to Sheffield as a pedlar. We know something of his later life from historical sources. In the 1881 census for Sheffield, he and Sarah, by now in their early 60s, were living at 56, Infirmary Road, with Teasdale's profession recorded as 'lecturer'. By this time *Life and Adventures* was in its twentieth edition. Sarah died two years later, and in 1886 Teasdale married his second wife, Ann. They lived together for sixteen years before his death. Teasdale enjoyed a remarkably long life considering his propensity for fast living and heavy drinking; he died in 1904 aged 86 at Fir Vale Workhouse Asylum, where he had been interred two weeks previously due to a 'malady of the mind'.[10] He is buried in Sheffield's General Cemetery.

Life and Adventures provides a rare, first-hand account of Victorian

6   *Sheffield & Rotherham Independent*, 'The Man Monkey in a New Character', 24th January, 1865; *Sheffield & Rotherham Independent*, 'The Hallelujah Band' letter to the editor by Harvey Teasdale, 2nd February, 1865.

7   Sheffield & Rotherham Independent, 'The Hallelujah Band' letter to the editor by 'Anti-Humbug', 25th January, 1865.

8   *The Era*, 'Our Omnibus', 7th May, 1871.

9   *The Era*, 'Topics of the Week', 17th September, 1871.

10   *Sheffield Daily Telegraph*, 'Death of a Noted Sheffield Character', 6th June, 1904.

working-class life writing. Told from Teasdale's highly entertaining and dramatic perspective, the world of working-class Sheffield comes to life, his story unfolding between seedy dealings and narrow escapes. The narrative traces his experiences on the stage, ranging from roadside performances to engagements with Sheffield's grandest theatres. Punctuated with humorous anecdotes and proud asides, the conversion narrative he sets out to tell undulates between pious pleas and exciting reminiscences. Teasdale confesses his sins and his successes, omits dates and information where he sees fit, quoting heavily from the Bible while promoting his performing skills. Indeed, his confession generates more secrets and further intrigue. Teasdale uses literary references, archaic terms, and lengthy sentences in an attempt to refute the class-based expectation that his writing skills will be limited. What becomes clear is how much *Life and Adventures* stands out as a working-class autobiography written by a man striving to make a life for himself beyond his origins. Periodically, Teasdale drops out of his first-person narrative and speaks about himself in the third person: 'Harvey Teasdale was not to be affronted'; 'it was prophesied by one of the Walkley belles that Harvey would become an actor'. Slipping into the third person allows Teasdale to comment on his own life from an outside perspective, repeating and promoting his own name, revelling in his own successes. Teasdale's approach to life writing and unique perspective of Victorian Sheffield, theatrical performance, fame, alcoholism, incarceration, confession, and conversion make *Life and Adventures* an invaluable, individual account of an often overlooked sector of society.

TIMELINE

1817 Harvey is born

c.1830 Establishes Juvenile Amateur Society

Early 1830s Establishes Amateur Theatrical Society

Mid 1830s Recruited to a travelling theatre near Retford (Nottinghamshire)

Mid-late 1830s Marries Sarah

1838 First daughter, Sarah Ann Teasdale, born

1842 Second daughter, Harriett Teasdale, born

Early 1840s Performs with travelling booth companies such as Douglass's and Thorne's

24th March 1845 Appears in front of the magistrates charged with abandoning family

Mid to late 1840s Begins performing as 'man monkey'; can be traced as an actor and manager around East Anglia, the Midlands, northern England and Scotland

Christmas 1847 First dubbed 'Herr Teasdale' during engagement at Queen's Theatre, Manchester

1852-3 Spends a number of prosperous months at Grimsby (Lincolnshire)

1858 Final performance in London as the clown in *King Comet*

1859-1860 Manages Theatre Royal in Huddersfield (Yorkshire)

1860-1862 Isolated engagements at Manchester, Liverpool, and Cardiff

1861 Census shows Harvey, Sarah, Harriett, and Ann living at separate addresses

4th August 1862 Attacks wife and attempts suicide; sentenced to two years in Wakefield Prison

9th November 1864 Released from prison

25th December 1864 Props and costumes advertised for sale in the *Era*

Late 1860s Autobiography first published

1869 5th edition of autobiography published

1881 Census shows Harvey and Sarah living together at 56, Infirmary Road, Sheffield; Harvey's occupation is 'lecturer'; autobiography has gone into 20th edition and sold 42,000 copies

1883 Sarah Teasdale dies

1886 Marries second wife, Ann

1891 Census shows Harvey and Ann living together at 263, Moorfields, Hillsborough; Harvey listed as a 'fishing tackle dealer'

1901 Census shows Harvey and Ann still living at 263, Moorfields; still a 'fishing tackle dealer'

June 1904 Harvey dies in Fir Vale Workhouse Asylum

NOTE ON THE TEXT

We have transcribed the text as it was published, according to the 1881 edition. However, in the few instances where Teasdale's syntax is particularly complicated, or his spelling erroneous, we have made slight adjustments in order to clarify his meaning. In the footnotes, where possible, we have identified the people and places mentioned by Teasdale, and the phrases and quotations he uses.

ACKNOWLEDGEMENTS

We would like to thank Dr Jack Windle and Dr Amber Regis for their assistance and support throughout the project. We could not have undertaken this research without the support of the Sheffield University Research Experience (SURE) funding scheme, and the University of Bristol's Kathleen Barker Archive. Funding was also received from the University of Sheffield and the *Arts Council for England* for additional research and the development of a performance based on the life of Harvey Teasdale, which premiered at the 2014 *Festival of the Mind*. This performance was undertaken in collaboration with Point Blank Theatre Company, Sheffield, and we are particularly grateful to Steve Jackson and Amy Beard for their creative input.

ABOUT THE EDITORS

Rosie Whitcombe is coming to the end of her second year of PhD study at Birmingham City University. She completed her undergraduate degree in English Literature in 2015, and her masters in Nineteenth Century Studies in 2016, both at the University of Sheffield. Rosie's current research focuses on the letters of Romantic poet John Keats. Her thesis will provide a new historical and critical account of letter writing with a focus on self-fashioning, theories of the epistolary and the text as artefact.

She is particularly interested in the specific tensions that arise in epistolary relationships and how Keats creates and destabilises notions of the self in his correspondence. Rosie first encountered Harvey Teasdale in 2014 during her penultimate year of undergraduate study. She received funding through the SURE (Sheffield University Research Experience) scheme to assist Professor Dawn Hadley, Dr Vicky Crewe, and Point Blank Theatre Company with their ongoing research into *Life and Adventures*. Rosie is interested in the overlapping confession and conversion narratives in *Life and Adventures* and what Teasdale's appropriation of various literary texts and forms can tell us about the autobiography as a genre.

Dawn Hadley is Professor of Medieval Archaeology at the University of York, and was formerly a professor in the Department of Archaeology at the University of Sheffield. Her research interests are principally the Viking Age, medieval gender, childhood and funerary practices, and she has published many books and articles on these topics. However, she has also developed research interests in the nineteenth century in recent years, especially working-class culture. The emergence of this new research area began unexpectedly when she was excavating the medieval hunting lodge in Sheffield in collaboration with Vicky Crewe and they uncovered extensive evidence of the mining community that occupied the ruins of the lodge in the nineteenth century. It was through the research that they subsequently undertook on Victorian Sheffield that they came across the intriguing autobiography of Harvey Teasdale. In 2014 they worked with Sheffield's Point Blank theatre company to develop a play about Harvey Teasdale, which was performed at the University of Sheffield's *Festival of the Mind*. Dawn has a long track record of public engagement, and the play and the publication of this annotated version of Teasdale's autobiography are among numerous examples of the ways in which she has sought to bring academic research to a wider public audience and readership.

Vicky Crewe is a historical archaeologist whose most recent research explores the post-medieval world, particularly material culture, domestic life, popular culture, empire and childhood in the nineteenth century. Whilst working on the project 'Performing the Past: Exploring the Heritage of Working-Class Communities in Yorkshire', she and Dawn encountered the autobiography of Harvey Teasdale. Vicky is particularly interested in how Teasdale's memoir – especially his descriptions of his childhood escapades – reveal a personal geography of nineteenth-century Sheffield and how this enriches what we learn from 'factual' sources such as maps. In other projects, Vicky has researched how toys and games were used during and after the Second Boer War to influence children's attitudes to national identity and the British Empire, and investigated how 'family archives' communicate between generations. Her research draws on photographic, documentary and literary records and archaeological sources, and she has collaborated widely with other academics, activists, museum curators, archivists and public audiences. Vicky has held research, teaching and public engagement roles at the University of Sheffield and Cardiff University, and currently works in learning and teaching development at the University of Sheffield.

The
Life and Adventures
of
Harvey Teasdale,
The Converted Clown
and
Man Monkey,
with his
Remarkable Conversion in
Wakefield Prison.

Written by himself.

Twentieth Edition. Forty-second Thousand.

Entered at Stationer's Hall. The Right of Translation Reserved.

SHEFFIELD

C. Leonard and Son, Steam Printing Works Wicker.

1881.

PREFACE

In publishing this history of my life's experience, I am influenced only by the thought that, as the relation of it in the form of addresses in Sheffield and the surrounding villages has been attended with manifest proofs of the Divine favour in the conversion of many precious souls during the delivery, the publishing of it in this extended and consecutive order, may, by the same Divine blessing, be followed by an equal enlarged measure of success.

Your friend in Jesus Christ,
HARVEY TEASDALE.

THE DARK SIDE

CHAPTER I

I was born in Sheffield Park, in 1817. I had very kind parents. My father was a spring knife manufacturer, and had I only followed the good advice of my pious mother, what misery I might have escaped. As soon as ever I was able to understand anything, my mother taught me that beautiful prayer—

> *Gentle Jesus, meek and mild,*
> *Look upon a little child.*[1]

She used to talk to me of Jesus, but I was too full of the follies of this world to think of the next. The poet says that "the child is the father of the man," and the following facts very forcibly illustrate this truth.[2] Before I could walk, I crept into mischief. One washing day my mother had taken out the oven plate to make room for the pansion[3] to boil the clothes in. The plate was put on the floor. In a moment I was on it; then commenced a row. My mother said, "do quiet that lad," but that was sooner said than done. They threatened, but still the crying went on. At last my mother came with the intention of warming my back, but she found I had done that myself, for I was stuck fast to the plate, the skin

---

1   Throughout the footnotes, we have provided where possible a reference to the texts Teasdale is referring to, although we cannot be sure which edition, if any, he consulted, nor from where his knowledge of various texts derived, bar what he claims in his manuscript. Charles Wesley, 'Hymns for Children', *Hymns and Sacred Poems* (1742) ('Gentle Jesus, meek, and mild,/Look upon a Little Child,/Pity my Simplicity,/Suffer me to come to Thee'), p. 194.

2   William Wordsworth, 'The Rainbow' or 'My Heart Leaps Up', *The Poetical Works of William Wordsworth* (London: Routledge, 1862), p. 1.

3   Teasdale is probably referring to a pancheon, a multi-purpose earthenware vessel, wider at the top than the bottom.

giving way with it. I have often heard my mother and sister speak of this. I remember a circumstance which happened when I was only about two years of age. We kept a grocer's shop at the top of Broad Lane, opposite where St. George's Church now stands. One day I saw my mother fetch flour out of a bin in the shop, so I got a stool and climbed up to the bin top, but, overbalancing myself, I fell headlong into the flour. You may be sure there was a row in the bin, upon hearing which, my mother came and fished me out, nearly smothered, but I was quieted by being permitted to ride in the miller's cart, which stood at the door. Now, I remember this as if it only happened yesterday, although I was so young. Many have questioned this, but it is the truth.

I next remember living at West Bank, West Street; my father had workshops there. One day, whilst playing in the bottom shop, a door, which opened into a deep cellar where my father kept his steel, was left ajar, and, as I was leaning against it, flew open, sending me headlong down the steps. One piece of steel that was reared against the wall cut open my cheek, and laid me on a sick bed for many weeks, but no sooner had I got out of doors again than I was in another scrape. At this time I was sent to the Carver Street National School, but I seldom went unless my sisters took me. Often, instead of attending to my schooling, I went down to the Wicker Bridge, running up to my neck in the water, with my clothes on, to amuse the blacksmiths who worked at the water-side, and who used to give me half-pence for this trick. When it was near the time for school to close, I would run up to Sanderson's furnace wall, in West Street, and lean against it till my clothes were dry, and then go home as if I had been at school. The school wage was paid weekly, but I often spent mine in sweetmeats instead of paying it, and when found out, I got a double thrashing – one from my father and another from the schoolmaster, who would also put me in the 'haunted room'; this was next to the front entrance. To frighten the other scholars, they were told that the devil's club-foot was on the ceiling, and that the room was haunted. I know this, that it was not long haunted with my presence, for no sooner had the door been locked and the master gone to his desk, than I climbed up to the window, lifted it up, and bolted off down to my old rendezvous, the Wicker Dyke. Of course, for this I received the double dose of flogging, which did not trouble me much as I had got hardened to it. Now, they thought to put a stop to my pranks of leaping

out the window, so they found another prison for me. At the top of the
boy's school was a very large oven, so they put me into it and fastened the
door upon me. Now, this suited me – I liked it better than going to the
Dyke; so I commenced running and squeaking about the oven – kicking
up such a noise that set all the boys in the school in a roar, and the master
was obliged to acknowledge he was beaten, and glad to let me out. He
sent word to my parents that they had better keep me at home, for he
could do nothing with me. I used to be very fond of running up spouts,
and getting on to roofs of buildings, and running on the slates like a cat.
One day I had run up a spout in West Bank; when I got on to the top, the
spout, being rotten, gave way, and down fell both I and the spout. The
people thought I was killed, but, bless God, He did not cut me off. For
days I was insensible, and was laid up for weeks; but all the time, instead
of making up my mind to do different, I was longing for the time when
I should be able to get out and be at my tricks again.

I still went to the Carver Street Sunday School, when I could not
help it – that is, when my sister took me. At this time the scholars went
to the Hospital Chapel, which was situated underneath where the Corn
Exchange now stands; it was a round building, which eventually became
a circus. One Sunday I fell asleep whilst the sermon was going on, and
slept until all the congregation had left the chapel. I was awakened by
the banging to of one of the doors, and, finding myself alone in the
chapel, I was in a fearful fright. I rushed down the stairs into the yard,
and up the steps into the street running up Dixon's Lane. When at the
top, I discovered I had left my new seal cap in the chapel, so I had to
go back and get the chapel-keeper to fetch it for me, which he kindly
did, and away I went. I had reached the bottom of Bow Street, when
I saw two boys fighting – one much bigger than the other, though the
little one was bigger than myself. Seeing the little one getting punished,
I stopped him and said, "He is too big for you, let me have a go at him."
It was settled in a minute; then off went my new jacket and cap, which
I gave into the hands of a boy and commenced fighting, and very soon
beat my man. When the fight was over, I turned round to look for the
boy with my clothes, but he had bolted, clothes and all. This put me in
a fix; I dared not go home without my jacket and cap, as they were new
on that day. Some of the bystanders went home with me, to try to save
me from a thrashing, but they did not succeed; I got a fearful beating,

and I deserved it. I do not think at that time there was a lad in Sheffield, a stone heavier than myself, could stand any chance with me at fighting, and there scarcely passed a day without their having to test my fighting abilities.

My father had several apprentices; amongst them were two brothers of the name of Wroe, one of them, named William, was one of the most honest servants my father ever had, and a good workman, but both brothers were fearful blasphemers, and very passionate men; it was awful to hear them curse and swear; it was dangerous to be near either of them when these fits of passion were on them. One day William was squaring some blade tangs, and they were very hard; his tongue was thrust into his cheek, and his eyes nearly came out of their sockets with passion. If the blade maker had been there I would not have given much for his life. At that moment, a big fly came buzzing about his face; he cursed, it and kept making a stroke at it with the file, but missed it; still it buzzed about. At last, bursting into a fearful rage, he chased the fly round the shop, striking away, until the file flew out of the haft right through the shop window (panes cost a trifle in those days); he then sat down on the stone, frothing at the mouth. One day the other brother was cooking some beefsteaks on the shop fire, and the fire being very low, they were a long time doing; he kept going to look at them, each time with an oath; at last, in a dreadful passion, he seized the fire-grate with both hands, which, being a little one and loose, soon gave way; he then dragged it to the middle of the floor, threw it down with an oath, saying, "cook there." In a minute or two he was a corpse, having broken a blood-vessel. He had lived without Christ, and died without Him. Reader, are you in this state? Is Christ outside? If so, you are in great danger – your death may be as sudden as this poor man's. Death is certain, and after death judgment! Think of this, dear reader, and may God convert you, and save you. William Wroe lived a miserable life, and died a wicked death; he committed suicide by drowning himself in Crookes Moor Dam. "The wages of sin is death."[4] He served the devil all his life, and died in his service.

We had another apprentice – how different his end to theirs – his name was Abraham Hague, he lived with us at the same time as the Wroes did. I never knew the parents of the Wroes, but I did know the mother of

4   *The Bible: Authorised King James Version*, Romans 6:23 (Oxford: Oxford University Press, 1997). All further references will be attributed to this edition.

this man – good, pious, old Martha Hague; she lived in a little attic near my father's shop, and the day through you might hear her at her spinning wheel, for in that way she obtained her livelihood. This good old woman had been praying for her son, and God answered her prayer by saving her son, and bringing him to Himself. Abraham was a great martyr to the cramp; he suffered dreadfully with it. I have seen his poor face draw into most horrible shapes; at last it killed him, but he died in Christ. He went a little before his mother, and she knew she would meet him again to part no more. Old Martha was very fond of Harvey, and used to give me good advice, but it was like that given by my parents – it was not heeded, or I should have escaped years of misery. Old Martha soon followed her son, and now they are together, where I hope soon to join them.

After I was taken from the National School, in Carver Street, I was sent to the Netherthorpe Academy; it was situated at the top of Hoyle Street next to Lawyer Hoyle's Rookery.[5] In the play hours I used to be either up the trees upsetting the nests, or else stoning the crows, which set them cawing lustily. Old Lawyer Hoyle would come out cursing and swearing (and he could do it to some tune); with a stick in his hand, he would chase me over the fields, but would have to return out of breath without catching me. He would complain to Mr. Meggison, the school-master, who would give me a good caning. I used to amuse the scholars by leaping through hoops and over chairs like a monkey. Many of our best, as well as our worst, men went to this school; among the former was Mr. John Blake, merchant, Scotland Street, who was killed on the Midland Railway; Dr. Booth, Paradise Square; and in the latter, Cooper, who became notorious for breaking out of the Sheffield Lock-up. His father used to keep a low beer house in Bank Street. Many a thrashing has this Cooper received from me for telling the schoolmaster of my tricks. Many of the well-to-do shopkeepers in Sheffield I recognise as once being schoolmates. One day a woman was driving some cows past my father's yard in West Street, but the cows did not go fast enough for me, so I went to help them on a bit; the woman came behind me with a blackthorn stick, and hit me on the head with all her might, breaking in my skull, the blood spurting up a yard high from the wound. I was taken to the infirmary, and I well remember the doctor saying, "Don't cry, my man, and I'll give you twopence." I did not cry, and got the twopence. Now,

---

5   A breeding ground or nesting place for a flock of birds, not necessarily rooks.

the woman who had so near killed me was permitted to go unpunished, because my father would never prosecute anyone; he has had his shop robbed time after time, and known the thief, but would not have him sent to prison. I daresay my father thought I deserved all I got, and I believe he was right. I was serving Satan and he was paying me my wages.[6]

My father had several horses, and I was very happy when permitted to drive them in the cart. One day my father let me and a playmate of mine, named Bill Burton, who lived next door to the woman who kept the cows, of Little Hill, and who broke my head, go to Newbould's pit to fetch a load of coals. This same Burton I saw in Wakefield Prison, serving a short time, but it appears to have had no good effect on him. I often meet him in rags and idleness, preferring to serve his old Master, the devil, with misery and rags, to serving Christ, with comfort while on earth, and a glorious life hereafter. I pray to God to open his blind eyes, that he may see the dangerous ground he is walking upon, that he may flee from it to the safe rock, Jesus Christ, and be saved for time and eternity. But now, to return to my narrative. We had a quiet old horse in the cart, called Boxer; he was very slow, and not altogether sure. We had started off early in the morning, and a day of trouble we had of it. Poor old Boxer had a very naughty way of going on his knees, and when down was not easy to get up again. We reached the pit at Intake,[7] and after waiting our turn, got the coals and the ticket all right. A happy thing it will be, dear reader, for you and for me if, when death comes, we have got our ticket for heaven all right and properly endorsed – not having on our own righteousness, but the righteousness of Christ, the only passport, the Bible says, that will admit us to heaven. Off we started, and when we came out of the yard we had to come down a narrow lane, with very bad deep ruts; we had not got far before old Boxer was on his knees, and then all his length on the floor, and half of the coals out of the cart. Bill and I ran back to the yard, crying for someone to come and help us up with the horse. After a time Boxer was placed on his legs, the coals were

---

6　　Teasdale repeats this maxim throughout to emphasise how his actions were repeatedly met with punishment. It is probably inspired by several Biblical passages, such as the aforementioned 'The wages of sin is death' (Romans 6:23) as well as 'The labour of the righteous tendeth to life: the fruit of the wicked to sin' (Proverbs, 10:16), amongst others.

7　　Intake is a district of south-east Sheffield.

got into the cart again, and off we started once more, but had not gone far before down he went again, upsetting the cart, this time turning all the coals into the lane.

Burton and I had a swearing duet here – swearing had become a confirmed habit with me then. The Bible says for every idle word that a man utters he shall give an account – then what an awful amount of condemnation and punishment must accrue to the man who has gained – it may be insensibly – the wicked and depraved habit of swearing. I pray you, dear reader, shun it. It was late at night when we got to Sheffield; our folks thought we had got lost, and had sent someone to seek us. We were very glad to meet him, and willingly gave up old Boxer to his care, making our minds up never to go for coals with Boxer again. Poor old horse! I believe he used to fall asleep as he walked. My father sold him to Lord Sitwell,[8] to feed his hounds upon; and I very well remember when Jim Tomlinson, one of my father's men, took him out of the yard for the last time, on the way to Lord Sitwell's, just as he got out of the gates, he went down on his knees. Jim cried out, in the greatest terror, "Lord, have mercy upon me." After that Jim was content to walk, leading the poor horse to his fate. My father had a handsome little pony called "Captain." This pony could do almost anything; he was a great pet with all the family. Often, when my father had been coming home at night from Whiston, and other villages and towns around Sheffield, if he had been drinking, the pony knew it, and would walk slowly; and if my father happened to fall over into the road, which he did many a time, the pony would stop in a moment and whinny until someone came and picked him up, and often picked his pockets at the same time. Drink, the bane of the poor man, what souls it has sent to eternity, to realise the certain doom denounced in the Bible, that "no drunkard shall inherit the kingdom of heaven."[9] What cruel tricks it plays the victims, whom it first blinds and ultimately slays! What innocent children it has robbed, in many cases, of their rich inheritance! What families it has wholly engulfed in hopeless poverty! What, in my case even, would have been the difference it might have made in my after destiny had my father been a teetotaller.

8   The Sitwells were baronets of Renishaw Hall (Derbyshire); this is probably a reference to the second baronet, Lord George Sitwell (1797-1853).

9   An interpretation of 1 Corinthians 6:10 ('Nor thieves, nor covetous, nor drunkards, nor revilers, nor extortioners, shall inherit the kingdom of God').

About this time they opened the Hyde Park Cricket Ground as a race-course for ponies. Captain was entered, and would have won one race but for some blacklegs who bribed the jockey. Poor Captain! He died of mad staggers[10] in a field in Black Lamb's Lane, now known as Broomhall Street. But I am anticipating my story. My father was drinking one night in company with a butcher, who lived in Pea Croft. This man had an old screw of a horse, not worth a shilling; it was blind of[11] one eye, and could see very little out of the other; but that night my father was more blind than it with drink. The butcher told him it was a first-rate hunter (if it was not it was at least ready for the hounds) and a fast racer. This just suited my father, he wanted one very quick on his legs – I must say he was very fast on his legs, but it was at kicking. My father was about running a "Waterloo"[12] to Rotherham and Doncaster, and wanted a horse that would pass all on the road. The butcher said that he had got just the one to suit him, and he persuaded my father to give him the pony and five pounds in exchange for his bag of bones. When my father got up the next morning and knew what he had done, he was almost mad; but the deed was done. Drink, cursed drink, had done it. All the family fretted to part with the pony, and at the imposition which, through father's besetting sin, had been so shamefully practised upon him. However, the roguery of the butcher brought him very little profit, as the devil's wages seldom do, for the pony soon afterwards went mad, and died, as before stated, in Black Lamb's Lane.

My father very soon got a splendid "Waterloo" (a kind of round jaunt-ing car), and as Doncaster Races were coming on, he intended to run the "Waterloo" every day during the race week; one of my father's workmen was to drive it. It was usual for those carriages to stand in the Wicker, waiting for passengers. Well, there was our new carriage – looking the very prince of carriages – and the old blind screw with a brand new suit of

---

10 According to James White's *A Complete System of Farriery, and Veterinary Medicine* (Pittsburgh: Butler & Lambdin, 1818), p. 66, mad staggers was a dis-ease that could make a horse 'highly delirious, and so violent, that it is often dangerous to come near him. Sometimes he falls down, and appears to be quite exhausted; but, after a short time, he suddenly rises, and becomes as furious as at first. The only remedy for this disease is copious bleeding'.

11 i.e. 'in'.

12 Teasdale goes on to define a 'Waterloo' as 'a kind of round jaunting car'.

harness, intended to hide all defects, but, alas! hiding did not cure them, nor prevent those disastrous consequences sure to follow in their wake. Like many men I have known trying to hide their secret moral leprosy and wicked self-indulgences – hiding them by an outward semblance of morality – sometimes putting on the garb of religion, covering them with religious phrases, with charitable gifts, and so forth – covering, but not curing their moral leprosy; that can only be done by the renewing of God's Holy Spirit. Well, there stood our new enterprise, on which father had fixed his hopes. The horse, I fancy, was asleep, for, being blind, it could not be told when he was asleep. The carriage was soon filled with passengers anticipating a pleasant ride to the races; but, alas! for such airy visions, they had reckoned without their host. The old horse that was expected to carry them to their sport was asleep, probably dreaming of green fields or a well-filled fodder; but feeling the smarting application of the whip, he let fly with both his hind legs, and sent them through the front of the "Waterloo," squandering[13] the people in every direction, some screaming, some shouting to the horse to quieten him, but all to no purpose; the screw kept at his work, making chips of the new carriage front, and his mettle being now up, away he started with only the shafts, and certainly, as my father had said, passed all on the road, until he came to a full stop at the old Twelve o' Clock Tollbar with all the steam completely taken out of him. Not very long after he followed poor Boxer to feed Lord Sitwell's hounds, and all the money my father got for the lying butcher's horse, skin and bones, was the paltry sum of ten shillings.

One day my father sent me to Portobello Street, to reach which, from our house in West Street, I had to cross Marsh Field, which was situated at the back of Sanderson's Furnace (the place spoken of where I used to dry my clothes after my exploits at the Wicker Weir). The Marsh field was a cricket ground, but on the day that I was sent on this errand two men were playing a knur and spell match.[14] I, of course could not pass on without stopping to have a look at them; so intent was I upon the,

---

13 i.e. 'scattering'.

14 Also referred to as nurspell; an old English game, not unlike golf. The players take it in turns to hit the spell (a levered, wooden trap) to releases the knur – or knurr – (a small ball) and hit it with the kibble (a bat). The art of the game is to strike the knur with the kibble before it reaches the ground, and whoever drives it to the greatest distance, wins the game.

to me, exciting scene, that I had forgot all about my errand and whilst standing behind the striker, received Satan's pay for my idleness by a stroke which was intended for the knur, but it hit my cheek instead, which sent me spinning like a top. Talk about having a cheek for this or that: I, unfortunately, had a cheek as large as a child's head, and well was it for me that it was my cheek and not my eye that was struck. And oh! is there no Providence, dear reader, in these "accidents", as some people call them? The devil was permitted to punish me for my idleness and disobedience to parental commands – but then he might have taken my eye; yet God, who says to Satan "hitherto shalt thou go and no further,"[15] continued to me the use of my eyes, for which I bless His preserving care, and adore the eternal council that so wonderfully and mercifully arranges and presides over our everyday life. When I got home the only sympathy I received from my father was that I was not punished bad enough; in that, however, I differed from him – I was convinced I had had enough.

At another time, being sent by my father for some blades, I took the opportunity of seeking that rendezvous for idle boys – Green Lane Dyke, where, but for the interposition of that same Providence which the sceptic though himself largely sharing its blessings, so impiously ignores and derides, I should then have ignominiously closed my early career of idleness and sin. Seeing some bigger boys than myself going up to their necks in the water, I ventured to follow, and not being able to swim, I got beyond my depth, and was with difficulty saved from a watery grave, proving the truth of the saying, "That a man's immortal till his work is done." God had a work for me to do, and to prepare me for it has passed me through the rough discipline of the devil's wages in sin's hard tread-mill, where there are "more kicks than half-pence," and where I have been made to feel how dreadful a thing it is to sin against God. Fellow sinner, why should you, a posherd[16] of the earth, strive against your Maker? What can you hope to gain by it? What have I gained by it? Can you hope to escape the miserable consequences of sin here, or the penal doom of endless misery hereafter? Pray earnestly to be reconciled to God.

The next day-school I went to was Fox's, in Norfolk Street. For a time I got on well, but I soon began my old tricks again. "Can a negro change

---

15 Job 38:11 ('Hitherto shalt thou come, but no further').

16 Teasdale means potsherd or potshard, a fragment of broken pottery.

his skin, or a Leopard his spots?"[17] So my propensities again displayed themselves in performing all sorts of monkey tricks – upsetting the ink on the scholars' copy books, rubbing out the boys' sums from the slates; none daring to tell, for I was the terror of the school. The schoolmaster was fond of a nap in the afternoon, and once, when he was asleep, I pinned his coat-tail to the stool on which he sat. A noise at the other end of the school awoke him. Angry at his being thus suddenly disturbed, and anxious to punish the unfortunate offender, he started from his seat. The sudden jerk brought the stool in heavy contact with his legs, which made him shriek with pain, and set the whole school in a roar of boisterous and uncontrollable laughter. A searching investigation took place to ascertain the real culprit, threatening to flog all round if no confession was made, but my influence was so great in the school that, though the flogging was carried out *seriatim,*[18] it remained undiscovered who was the real offender. Annoyed that the whole school should be innocently punished, I promised to avenge them, so I knocked a needle through the bottom of the stool on which he used to sit. The scholars were all watching in high glee for the success of the scheme; they had not long to wait. The unsuspecting schoolmaster went to the desk, sat down with a toss, and as quickly sprang up again, with a countenance so ludicrously contorted that, but for the fear of again being punished, would have produced a burst of laughter. Prudence with these lads was the better part of valour, and so they restrained their mirth. The schoolmaster, with prescience peculiar to his profession, singled me out, saying, in look at least, "Harvey, I shall not ask you if you have done it, but I'll make you at least the scapegoat;" and thus it was I that got a caning which I richly deserved.

At this time there was a family living at Gleadless,[19] who worked for my father, named Law. One of the sons was called Joe, who afterwards became a notorious prize-fighter, and celebrated amongst the fighting fraternity – a class of men about as far removed from the reach of saving grace as any portion of the community but, which God has shown, can, and have been, reclaimed by His unlimited Mercy, and scores of them have lately been made monuments of His redeeming grace. If any of my

---

17 Jeremiah 13:23 ('Can the Ethiopian change his skin, or the leopard his spots?').

18 A series of floggings.

19 A district of south-east Sheffield.

readers belong to this class, let me say, "Don't be afraid to yield to the strivings of His grace – there is no dishonour in yielding to such an adversary as the mighty Saviour." Many a prouder and stronger man has said

> *I yield, I yield,*
> *I can hold out no more;*
> *Constrained, by dying love compelled,*
> *Jesus! I own thee conqueror.*[20]

But to return. Joe and I quarrelled over some birds, and we fought a pitched battle for two hours; neither of us would give in. The bystanders at last parted us. We shook hands and became fast friends, and backed each other in many an after fight.

My father, seeing it was very little use sending me to a school in Sheffield, and thinking to draw me away from my companions and haunts, sent me to a boarding school at Dronfield,[21] about seven miles from Sheffield. The country suited me; I could now romp to my heart's content, and practice my favourite pastime of bird-nesting. For a time I got on well, won several prizes at school, and should have got on much better, but that the schoolmaster, James Watts, was very fond of his beer, and though classed amongst moderate drinkers, did occasionally go to extremes, and then neglected his school for days together. Going over to Sheffield – of course, on business, which business was not in Minerva's grove or mart, but in that of Bacchus – often kept him for days together, when he would come back greatly fatigued by the pressure of engagements, and had to renew his strength, poor man, by lying in bed for a day or two. This gave me an opportunity of which I was glad to avail myself, by indulging my idle and wandering propensities in the fields. It was on one of these occasions which the only noble act that I can in anyway be proud of occurred. A woman, who kept a little spice or confectioner's shop on the Chesterfield Road, went to pass a few hours with some friends who resided at the top of town. Going from her home to those friends she had to cross a bridge at the low side of Lucas's dam. When she crossed in the afternoon the dam was, as usual, all right, but

---

20 Charles Wesley (1707-1788), 'The Resignation', *Hymns and Sacred Poems,* 1740 ('Nay, but I yield, I yield!/I can hold out no more;/I sink, by dying love compell'd,/And own thee Conqueror').

21 in Derbyshire.

when she returned at night the dam had overflowed, and the water was rushing over the bridge. The poor woman was ignorant of this, and, it being dark, she attempted to cross the bridge; the water carried her off her feet down the stream. She screamed for help. I happened to be on the road, heard her cries and rescued her from a watery grave. She asked me to go home to her house, and she would reward me. I went, and received a "spice bullseye,"[22] sold at a farthing – an appreciation of her own value not very flattering to herself, but which, at the time, I thought was as much as it was worth.

I stayed at Dronfield all the summer, but when winter came, I became dissatisfied, especially because I had to go to Coal Aston every morning at six o'clock to fetch milk, a duty which was very repugnant to my feelings; and so one afternoon, without notice, and without my cap, I got on to the back of the Nottingham mail coach and so reached Sheffield. When I got home they were washing. Old Betty, the washerwoman, when she saw me, called out to my mother "Oh, dear! here's Harvey come back without his cap!" My mother scolded me, and said she was afraid father would kill me when he came home, so she sent me upstairs out of the way. When father came home to his tea, and was told of my return, he flew into a violent passion, and exclaimed in his fury, "Limb of the devil, I'll kill him!" He went into the workshop, and got a heavy stick to thrash me with. I heard all that passed, and prepared myself accordingly. I went upstairs and put the bolster into the bed, covering it with my clothes, as though it was myself that was in the bed, and when I heard my father on the stairs, coming up, I crept under the bed. Luckily, my father came up without a candle, and commenced thrashing the bolster, I groaning and crying, but laughing heartily in my sleeve at my trick. When my father thought he had given me enough, he went downstairs again; I jumped into bed. My mother soon came in after with a basin of hot tea to heal my sore bones, and spoke kindly to me, hoping that the severe thrashing I had received would be a warning to me. My mother's kind words did more to soften my heart than my father's severity, and under this influence, I inwardly promised to do better; but where grace is not, these good resolutions are like the morning cloud and the early dew – they soon pass away.

---

22 A hard-boiled striped sweet, often peppermint flavoured, similar to a humbug.

CHAPTER II

It was now determined by my parents that I should go to school no more. I was to commence working as a cutler under my father. Most of my time was spent in running errands. The Cutlery business consists of many parts and processes, and necessitates a good deal of running about after the material, from grinders and others. Unfortunately for those concerned, I had a sad propensity of stopping on my way to and from the workshop, which caused the men to lose much time, and became a great annoyance to my father. One day I was sent for some blades, which ought to have taken me an hour to go there and back, but having had two fights on my way there, and spent some time fishing in a stream at the bottom of a garden belonging to the man to whom I had been sent for the blades, more than two hours were gone, and Harvey had not made his appearance. My father was tired of waiting, and came to meet me. He found me stripping to fight with a boy much bigger than myself who had been stealing some horse dung which I had gathered on the road. My father told me to put on my coat, and said if I wanted a thrashing he would do it when he got me home. The boy, seeing this, began to chaff and ridicule me. This annoyed my father, upon seeing which I urged my father to let me fight him. My father said, "Do you think you can beat him?" "Certainly," I said; so I got his permission, which pleased me much, because my father would now be a spectator of my prowess, and I determined to do my best, which proved more than a match for my antagonist, and gave me a triumph of which I was not a little proud, compelling my boasting antagonist quickly to strike his colours and make a very speedy exit. And thus I saved myself from a thrashing which my father had threatened to give me when I got home.

I was sent some time after this to the Union Wheel for some blades from the grinders,[23] and, having to wait for them finishing, I strolled into Cook Wood, bird-nesting – my favourite pastime. Again the evil destiny

23 Teasdale is probably referring to the Union Grinding Wheel, a grinding mill in the Netherthorpe area of Sheffield.

which dogged my steps, and threatened ever and anon to cut short my ill-starred youth, once more prevailed. My attention was attracted to a nest on a very high tree, which some boys were vainly attempting to get. A stone, which a boy had thrown at the nest, had lodged in one of the topmost boughs; in ascending the tree the stone, having become loosened, fell on my head and pierced the skull, from which the blood flowed freely. A crowd soon gathered quickly to convey my unconscious form home to a grieved mother, whom my conduct had so very often made sad and sorrowful. No sooner did my dear mother see the crowd than she, with maternal instinct, cried, "It's Harvey again – I'm sure it is!" True, dear mother, I was serving the devil, and he was thus paying me my wages. What can anyone expect in serving a master whose only aim is to produce all the misery and suffering which his victims are capable of enduring, and whose rage is provoked because of the limits which a most merciful Saviour has graciously prescribed? But now having gained admittance into that fold from which this prowling wolf is excluded, I, and the people with whom I am now united, can sing—

We are a garden, walled around,
Chosen and made peculiar ground:
A little spot, enclosed by grace,
Out of the world's wild wilderness.[24]

Sometime after the above, I was sent to a grinding wheel, called the Screw Mill, for some scissor knives that were sent to be polished. Near this wheel there was a heap of rubbish – the sweepings of the different hulls – around which the unemployed and idle lads would assemble to rummage in search of stray blades, &c. Of course I must join in the search, so I put down my knives and cap, and entered into the sport with such zest that I was almost oblivious of a fact which, when I did become conscious of it, made me fit to curse the day on which, it then appeared to me, I was so unluckily born, for, whilst thus engaged in searching for

---

24 Isaac Watts (1674-1748), 'The Church the Garden of Christ', *Hymns and Spiritual Songs* (c.1709). Taken from Selma L. Bishop *Isaac Watts: Hymns and Spiritual Songs 1707-1748. A Study in Early Eighteenth Century Language Changes* (Glasgow: The Faith Press, 1962) p. 71. ('We are a Garden wall'd around,/Chosen and made peculiar Ground;/A little Spot inclos'd by Grace/Out of the World's wide Wilderness').

other people's lost blades, I lost my own blades, or rather my father's, and they were very expensive ones; someone had both stolen them and my cap. Here then was a pretty fix. I thought I was the most unlucky lad in existence, and others might think so too; that is a mistake that many people fall into, but that is only a blind to hide those serious faults of character which are alone the parents of those misfortunes which we are apt to attribute to inevitable necessity, but they are really the results of our own misconduct. If you, dear reader, would avoid these misfortunes, seek the protection of that Jesus who is the Saviour of all men, but especially of them that believe.

About this time my parents removed from Sheffield to Walkley Hall, and in this new sphere I soon proved to the lads at Walkley that Harvey Teasdale was not to be affronted with impunity, for in every engagement with the would-be-heroes of Walkley I was declared the victor. Here there commenced a new phase of my life and character which was destined to exercise so potent an influence on my entire future career. A little before Christmas myself and a few of my companions formed a company of "mummers."[25] I took the part of Hector, and soon became a good combat fighter, gaining great applause, with an abundance of pocket money; and in this capacity it was prophesied by one of the Walkley belles that Harvey would become an actor. Certainly, the germ of my new profession was now sown, and its fruits for good or for evil became quickly developed. The new character, which I had begun to relish, filled me with a thirst for theatrical performances, and soon after, for the first time, I went to the Theatre Royal, Sheffield. The play on this occasion was "George Barnwell," and was supposed to point out the evil of sin, to convey a good moral, and to be of great benefit to the rising youth.[26] I have had great reason, in the course of my life, seriously to question the beneficial influence of any play or tragedy whatever. A passing feeling or tear of sympathy may follow the touching scenes exhibited on the stage by a clever company, presided over by the genius of a Siddons, a Garrick, or a Kean,[27] but such evanescent feelings are neutralised by the vicious

---

25 Traditionally an amateur theatrical troupe who perform folk tales wearing masks.

26 George Lillo (1693-1739), *The London Merchant: The Tragedy of George Barnwell*, first performed in 1731.

27 Sarah Siddons (1755-1831), David Garrick (1717-1779), Edmund Kean

and immoral influence necessarily connected more or less with every theatre. The only impression which the play of "George Barnwell" created in my own mind was a strong desire to become an actor, and soon after I contrived to form a Juvenile Amateur Society for spouting favourite characters.

CHAPTER III

The following facts will show what a very little moral influence was exerted on my own mind and character by the play of "George Barnwell," which was intended, it is said, to warn the young from the insidious growth of covetousness and dishonesty. My father had two apprentices about my own age – Charles Smith and George Atkin. We had workshops both at Sheffield and Crookes Moor Side, and in going to our work it was a common thing for us to rob the gardens on our way, getting up very early in order to do so, and very few gardens escaped. On one occasion, whilst we were all three engaged in our nefarious work, it was Atkin's place to look out for the watchman, but instead of doing so, he was in another garden getting gooseberries. The owner of the garden, who lived in a house adjoining, heard us, and called out to us to know what we were doing. With a bravado, which was a strong trait in my character, I told him the truth, that we were only getting some pears (in fact, we had nearly filled a sack). The man replied, "Wait a bit, and I'll help you," an injunction which, of course, we thought there would be greater wisdom in the breach than in the observance. No time was lost in making our escape from the garden. The difficulty of getting away with the pears was not trifling; a thorn hedge through which I passed bore strong marks of the struggle, in which I left both my cap and not a little of the skin of my face. Charley Smith ran another way, calling out to Atkin, "quais, kiddy, there's a gauger." This was a password, a species of flash phrase, which we had originated for our mutual protection in emergencies of this nature. After I had gone a little way, in turning round a corner I ran against a watchman; down he went in a moment, but was quickly up again springing his rattle, and I as quickly started off again, leaving the sack of pears for the watchman

---

(1787-1833): successful actors of the eighteenth/early nineteenth century famous for their portrayals of Shakespearean characters.

to count, and finally I reached the shop, and thus escaped for this time, at least, that long arm of the law, which sooner or later visits on the head of the delinquent its certain and severest penalties.

"George Barnwell" had miserably failed to cure or even check that covetous spirit and love of adventure which was luring me on to the verge of that vortex of crime, into which many have sunk, never to rise again. It was not long after this that I had a fish poaching adventure, for which I had to taste what the law could do in compelling its victims to make atonement for its outraged honour. We – that is Charley, George, and myself – went to fish in Crookes Moor Dam early in the morning, before the watchman, who was appointed to protect the fish in the dam from being stolen, had come on his beat. We had capital success that morning, and whilst in the midst of our sport the watchman came. Charley and George saw him and ran. Giving me the signal, I followed suit, leaving rods and lines behind us, but, not having seen the way the watchman was coming, I found I was running towards him. On discovering my mistake, I jumped over a wall, the watchman after me. I should, however, have escaped him had I not had to receive my wages from my master, the devil. I wore pumps, or slippers, and these stuck fast in the clay. Finding myself running without my slippers, and not relishing the loss of them, I returned for them, and thus fell into the hands of the watchman, who being a tall, powerful fellow, there was not the slightest chance of any escape, and he at once took me to the Water Company's Works, to whom the fish belonged, to be examined and dealt with as they thought proper. The fish that I had caught were in my hat, on my head. When asked what I had done with the fish, I said that I had caught none. The fish, that were still in my hat at that moment, jumped on my head, and appeared to my guilty conscience to say, "Harvey, what a liar you are." My hat was taken off, and the fish being there as evidence of my guilt, I was at once taken to the Town Hall, and locked up in one of those wretched cells, which I inwardly vowed should never be patronised by my presence again, and it required no small amount of money from my father to release me therefrom.

Shortly after this came the dreaded cholera, which struck down so many victims. I never look at that relic of its fatality – The Cholera Monument – without a shudder at my own narrow escape from its unrelenting fangs.[28] Had I succumbed to its power, my father would never have been able to put up a similar Monument to the one that I have seen there, on which is inscribed –

And when the first wild throb is past
Of anguish and despair,
To lift the eye of faith to heaven,
And know my boy is there.[29]

I suffered greatly from the attack, and to nothing but the miraculous display of God's mercy am I indebted for my recovery. I was given up by my friends, but redeeming love was watching over Harvey, who was yet to be a monument of its marvellous saving power.

Soon after my recovery, I became possessed with a passionate desire to see that wonder of the world, the great metropolis of our country, London; and, with another boy, named Charles Black, who was similarly inspired, we determined to try our fortunes, and seek in that city of untold gold the realisation of those dreams of wealth and splendour which were vividly dancing before the mirage of our imaginations. With threepence in our pockets, we started one morning, without acquainting anyone with our intentions, to walk to London, and which, without being particularly posted up in geography, we hoped to reach in two or, at most, three days. At the end of the first day we had got a few miles beyond Chesterfield, and, night coming on, the darkness began considerably to depress our spirits; the golden dream seemed somehow to fade rapidly from our enraptured gaze, and, as if to hasten its effect, the rain began to fall in torrents, and the conviction commenced irresistibly and simultaneously to be impressed on our minds that we had made a slight mistake in leaving a comfortable home on so stupid an errand. After a short consultation under a haystack, we determined to retrace our steps, and at once commenced the return journey. We had not proceeded far, however, before we met an Irish man with a thick cudgel in his hand,

28 In 1832 the cholera epidemic claimed the lives of over four hundred people in Sheffield. The cholera monument was erected in Norfolk Park in 1834 in memory of those who fell victim to the disease.

29 Dale, 'A Mother's Grief', *Moral and Sacred Poetry*, (Devonport: W. Beyers, 1829) ('Yet when the first wild throb is past/Of anguish and despair,/To life the eye of faith to heaven,/And think – my child is *there*'), p. 245.

whom we passed with a fear and trembling that might have been greater had we been cognisant of the fact that he had robbed and beaten a lawyer's clerk not an hour before, as we afterward heard. We reached home about three o'clock in the morning, weary and footsore, and soaked to the skin, with every trace of fortune-making London washed from our minds.

My readers will perceive from this history of my boyhood, that a foundation was laid, so thoroughly blighted and immoral, as to leave but little hope for that manly stability and moral integrity of character without which it is vain to expect a manhood in any way worthy of the name. It is true that there were elements of character, even in boyhood, that needed but a right direction – a true moral and spiritual basis to produce a life more in accordance and approximating more obviously to that highest type of humanity which is presented to us in the person and example of our Lord Jesus Christ.

My manhood commenced in the formation of an Amateur Theatrical Society. We gave performances once a week at the Black Beer Brewery, in Edward Street, now known as the Manor Castle. One night we had announced the play of "Raymond and Agnes, or the Bleeding Nun," but we had miscalculated our power;[30] we had no one to take the part of the Ghost – the Bleeding Nun. I was then courting my present wife and, after much persuasion, she consented to attempt the part, on the condition that if she failed I should take all the responsibility upon myself; but, again, another difficulty presented itself in the personal appearance of my wife. The idea of a stout buxom girl, with cheeks red as the rising sun, attempting to personate a ghost; but what difficulties will not genius surmount? We dressed her in white (of course without crinoline), together with an awful amount of whitening, to hide the roses from her cheeks. The time came at length for her to appear, and, alas! as quickly to disappear. Her entrance on the scene, that was to have produced universal quaking and the rising of the hair like "quills upon the fretful porcupine," was hailed with roars of laughter, and the cry, "Oh what a fat ghost!" This reception sent the blood so forcibly into her face that the whitening itself seemed to turn red, which further increased their laughter into a very hurricane of mirth; my wife could not stand that, but at once made her exit. This put an end to the play, and the audience then demanded their

---

30   A play based on Matthew Lewis's novel *The Monk: A Romance* (1796).

money back, but this we thought unreasonable, and with all the physical force we could muster drove them out of the house.

At another time we announced a grand display of fireworks, together with the play of "Don Juan."[31] A man of the euphonious and very characteristic name of Fogg acted the part of the Don, and whether himself in a fog, or wishing to create one, managed to ignite the fireworks, producing so violent an explosion that it scattered the audience in every direction, who never even returned to ask for their money back, but were glad to have escaped with their persons unscathed by the folly of the Spanish Don.

It will be seen at once that this state of things rendered necessary a migratory change. We could not expect to maintain our position long in one place, and so we opened another room in Bramall Lane, at a public-house opposite St. Mary's Church. Some curious scenes were enacted here, one of which, from its grotesque character and the rough usage to which we were subjected, may be of some interest to the reader, as it will serve to show that the life of an actor, especially in the low comedy line, was too much akin to the realms of darkness to have any good moral influence, or realise the idea of our greatest bard —

> *To hold a mirror up to virtue,*
> *And show vice its own image.*[32]

Alas! It was vice again in all its naked and revolting deformity. Would to God that parents were more alive to the true interests of their children, and prevent them from going to such demoralising sinks of iniquity. In the midst of our performances, a lot of roughs from Blind Lane, maddened by drink, came into the room and upset the performance. The stage was fixed over the brew-house, and a trap-door on the stage was right over a mash-tub. When the roughs became boisterous and obstreperous, they were remonstrated with by the actors. This just suited and answered their preconcerted purpose; they leaped on the stage and commenced right and left pitching into the actors. To escape the fury

31 An adaptation of the legend of Don Juan, fictional libertine and womaniser; a character who influenced the works of Mozart, Molière, and Lord Byron, to name a few.

32 Teasdale is probably referring to Shakespeare's *Hamlet* 3.2 ('to hold, as 'twere, the mirror/up to nature, to show virtue her own feature').

of our assailants, we lifted the trap-door and made a precipitate retreat, without our making even a parting bow to the audience, and altogether oblivious of the warm reception we were about to receive in the mash-tub into which we were so unceremoniously precipitated. The next morning presented such an appearance of black eyes and marred faces as never, I believe, graced before or since such a company of would-be-actors of modern drama. But what else could be expected from those who thought it no crime to spend the hallowed hours of the Sabbath in the unhallowed practice of rehearsals.

Our next room was in Bailey Field, opened by a negro, whom some of my readers will remember was called "Black Charley," nor was his character and life less black than his skin and name, nor less fitted for the situation as the keeper of a jerry shop[33] in such a neighbourhood. It was here that I took what was called a "benefit,"[34] and being advertised, it came to the knowledge of my parents, who might have demurred at the profession their son had chosen, but being told that I was likely to turn out a "star," they offered me no opposition, seeing that it was no use to thwart me, as I was fully bent on the pursuit. Expecting a crowded house, I took what might seem strange to some, for the first time in my life, a little drop of gin. This was done to stimulate and strengthen my nervous system, Oh! I remember how, like a thief I stole into Aldam's dram shop,[35] in Church Street, to buy the dram, and how, still more

---

33 The Beer Act (1830) lowered the price of beer and 'enabled any taxpayer to brew and sell beer' in their own home. This resulted in an influx of Jerry shops, or 'Tom and Jerry houses', small establishments (or, indeed, households) that sold beer. The name is derivative of "the drinking and socialising activities of two popular characters; Jerry Hawthorn, Esq. and Corinthian Tom, serialised by Pierce Egan in *Life in London: Day and Night Scenes*" (Simon J. Robinson and Alexandra J. Kenyon, *Ethics in the Alcohol Industry* (London: Macmillan, 2009), p. 18).

34 A supplemental performance after which Teasdale would have kept all or most of the proceeds to compensate for an insufficient salary. Benefit performances were often part of an actor's contract during the early Victorian period. Typically, an actor was permitted one benefit per year, after which their employer (usually a theatre company) could not take their usual cut of the proceeds, leaving it all to the actor.

35 An establishment in Sheffield where alcoholic beverages were served. A dram is a unit of liquid capacity.

like a thief, I skulked into St. James' Street, to drink it, looking carefully round to see that no one observed me. Such I believe, is the feeling with which the inward monitor in every man's breast resists the commence-ment of that habit of drinking the intoxicating dram, which creates in the constitution itself a craving for the miserable stuff that palsies the arm, bloats the countenance, and ultimately drowns the soul in ever-lasting perdition. The benefit was a great success – the house was crowded. The applause reached the ceiling, and crowned me, if not with golden, then at least with coppery honours.

One of the actors was John Turton, the very man that was the watch-man for the Water Company, and took me as I have said, to the Town Hall, for catching fish in his employers' dam. He played "Luke, the Labourer." It was his favourite character, and he played it well for an amateur; he had a splendid voice. But John Turton was destined to play a higher part in God's Great Drama of redemption; he has had his eyes opened to see the evil of sin and receive Christ as his only saviour.

The next house we opened in the theatrical line was the Queen, in Scotland Street, which was fitted up with scenery of a much better class than any we had hitherto been able to obtain. Here we performed, for the first time, a piece called "The Sea, the Sea" or "The Ocean Child."[36] In this piece was represented a storm at sea. The action of the waves was produced by a piece of painted canvas, under which, to give it undulat-ing motion, some boys were introduced, whose tumbling made the ris-ing waves. The pealing thunder was made by shaking a sheet of rolled iron, and the flash of the lightning by powdered resin thrown through a lighted lamp. The bowsprit of a ship was made to appear on the side wing of the stage, from which a sailor was lowering himself by a rope to rescue a woman and a child from a watery grave. The sailor had just reached the woman with the child in her arms, the storm was at its height a shout was heard as if from the heroic sailor – "She is saved! – she is saved!" – when lo, just at that moment, all the scenery came down with a crash, nearly smothering the poor woman and her doll, for it was nothing more. The audience scampered out, tumbling over each other in the scramble, and adding to the confusion by screams and groans. A more vivid, real cli-max to a storm, either on sea or land, was, I should think, never realised on any stage either before or since. Two of the men that composed this

36 We have been unable to track down this play.

dramatic club went out of existence under circumstances as tragical, if not more so, than any they had ever played on the mimic stage. "Truth is more wonderful than fiction,"[37] so says the poet, and is fraught with many forcible and more palpable lessons of instruction than are to be found in the most romantic and sensational stories that have ever graced the pages of our best writers of fiction. If the reflective faculties with which all men are gifted were but called into more perfect exercise, what wisdom, knowledge, and instruction would be derived from those common everyday illustrations which the providence of God affords us in the lives of our companions and compatriots in life. One of the two I have just mentioned became a dissipated character, and in one of his not very sober moods listed for a soldier, and, after a variety of discreditable events, was suddenly cut off, and thus, by evil habits, fulfilled the truth of the infallible testimony of Holy Writ – "That the wicked shall not live out half their days."[38] The other was, unfortunately, so constituted that whatever pleased his eye, he had a strong propensity to pilfer. It was a species of mania with him that was constantly bringing him into scrapes, sometimes of a very ludicrous character. I used to think it was so very natural to him that he really could not help it. Phrenologists would say that it was because the bump of acquisitiveness was so large that he could not control it, and that he was not properly responsible for his actions. But subsequent experience, and the reading of good authors, have proved to me that this is a mistake. Any propensity, however strong, is capable of being controlled. I know a barrister (now living) who had a very excitable temper and irritable disposition, so that, when he first commenced practising, it gave the opposing counsel a very decided advantage, and was so far injuring him in his profession, but he found he must either give up his practice or resolutely master the failing. He conquered the habit, and is now one of the most equable of men.

It is said of Socrates, the Grecian philosopher, that on one occasion

---

37 Teasdale seems to be misquoting Canto XIV, Verse CI, of Byron's *Don Juan* (1819-24): 'Tis strange, but true; for truth is always strange,/Stranger than fiction. If it could be told,/How much would novels gain by the exchange!/How differently the world would men behold!'.

38 An interpretation of Psalms 55:23 ('But thou, O God, shalt bring them down into the pit of destruction: bloody and deceitful men shall not live out half their days').

a man, professing the principles of Lavater,[39] came to the disciples of Socrates and told them that he could tell any man's character from the shape of his features. The disciples of Socrates, in order to test the truth of his theory, brought him into the presence of Socrates, without telling the man who Socrates was, and afterwards they asked him to describe his character. This the man did, by saying that he had never seen a face so remarkably developed and striking; that in his opinion the man was of a most vicious and execrable disposition – a man capable of committing any act of villainy, a licentious reprobate, possessing every bad quality without a redeeming feature. When the disciples heard this they laughed at the man, and told him that he never was more mistaken in his life; that, in fact the man was the very opposite of the character which he had described. They afterwards told Socrates what the man had said, laughing to scorn the man's pretensions. "Stop," said Socrates, "the man was right; I am what the man has described, but, by the power of philosophy, I have been able to overcome it, and I am now what philosophy has made me."[40] Let it not be said, therefore, that a man is not responsible for his actions because he has got a strongly developed one-sided organization. "What man has done, man may do,"[41] is a maxim as true in ethics as in any de-

---

39 A reference to Johann Caspar Lavater (1741-1801), the Swiss physiognomist who endeavoured to discover 'whether it be possible to explain the undeniable striking differences which exist between human faces ... Whether these signs can communicate the strength and weakness, health and sickness of the body; the folly and wisdom, the magnanimity and meanness, the virtue and vice of the mind' (Lavater, *Physiognomy; or the Corresponding Analogy Between the Conformation of the Features and the Ruling Passions of the Mind* (London: Cowie, Low, &c., 1826), p. 2).

40 According to William Godwin's *Lives of the Necromancers, Or, An Account of the Most Eminent Persons in Successive Ages, Who Have Claimed for Themselves, Or to Whom Has Been Imputed By Others, the Exercise of Magical Power* (London: Frederick J. Mason, 1834) pp. 12-13, the 'story of Socrates and the physiognomist is sufficiently known. The physiognomist having inspected the countenance of the philosopher, pronounced that he was given to intemperance, sensuality, and violent bursts of passion, all of which was so contrary to his character as universally known, that his disciples decided the physiognomist was a vain-glorious pretender. Socrates however presently put them to silence, by declaring that he had had an original propensity to all the vices imputed to him, and had only conquered the propensity by dint of a severe and unremitted self-discipline'.

41 According to *The Oxford Dictionary of Phrase and Fable* ed. by Elizabeth

partment of labour. Let no one, therefore, seek to evade his responsibility on account of defective organization, or because some bump or organ is so strongly developed that it cannot be controlled. The idiot alone is the only irresponsible being.

But to return to my narrative. This man had a propensity to pilfer so strong, that he could not go into a shop without taking out something that did not belong to him. Whilst walking with me down Scotland Street, on one occasion, we passed a fish shop at the top of Lambert Street; on the outside of the window was a board on which were some large codfish. I noticed one of these fishes, to my very great surprise, without any apparent means, suddenly slide away from the board. I turned to discover the cause of this phenomenon, and found to my dismay, that my companion had surreptitiously slipped it under his coat, and was making off with it towards Grindlegate. The imminence of my own personal peril, in apparent complicity with the theft, suggested to my mind instant flight as the only means of escape from a most unpleasant dilemma. Accordingly I ran down Lambert Street with an alacrity that would have made me the winner of any race with the most expert pedestrian. My companion, I afterwards learnt, was followed by the woman of the shop, the owner of the fish, shrieking out with all her might, "Stop thief – Stop thief!" and so closely following him, that to assist his flight he was compelled to throw the fish over a wall in one of the narrow passages through which he was threading his way. The woman, however, was not to be baulked of her prey. She soon succeeded in reaching him, and, seizing hold of the skirt of his coat, it was completely severed in the struggle. A crowd had now collected. My companion pleaded mistaken identity, and was indignant at the woman's audacity in charging him, so respectably attired, with the crime of so paltry a larceny, and so effectually did he plead his own cause, and so gentlemanly was his appearance, that the people cried shame on the woman for defaming so respectable a man, and for transforming his beautiful frock coat into so undignified a spencer. Of course, he escaped further annoyance, and returned to my house, for he lodged with me. I was about to rate him soundly for so nearly bringing me into trouble, but

---

Knowles (Oxford: OUP, 2005), p. 429, this saying 'is recorded from the mid 19th century, but there is a similar idea behind a comment (1723) of S. Cranston, recorded in G. S. Kimball *Correspondence of Colonial Governors of Rhode Island* (1902), "But as the Proverb is what hath been may be again"'.

when I saw his grotesque appearance, with his disfigured habiliments, and heard his account of the ludicrous result of his adventure, I could but laugh at the incident, as being only one of those peculiarities for which my companion was so remarkable.

But the adventure did not end here; my companion was doomed to receive a lesson he certainly did not anticipate, but which he was not very likely to forget all the rest of his life. He said to me "I mean to have that fish yet; I know where it is, and at the right time I will fetch it." But many a man, like the wicked Haman, spoken of in the life of Esther, the Queen, as recorded in the Bible, has found the truth of the quaint old saying, that "the wickedness of the wicked shall fall on his own pate."[42] So my companion also found to his own cost. The woman, whose fish was stolen, when she got home, wondering what he had done with the fish, surmised that he must have thrown it away somewhere in his flight so forthwith she got a lantern, and searched for the fish until she found it, and, with a woman's sagacity, she conjectured that the thief would return for his prize, and so she got a number of men with sticks to watch with her the approach of the thief seeking for his prey. She armed herself with a brush handle, determined to have personal revenge upon the would-be-considered gentleman, who she was sure was the veritable thief. She had not watched long before he made his appearance, stealthily groping his way in search of his supper, but instead of regaling himself with cod fish and sauce, he received such a dose of birch wood and broom-handle sauce, so hard to digest, that it nearly lost him his life. He did, however, manage to escape, with a hide and bones so sore and disfigured with bruises, that I verily believe this summary chastisement did more good in curing him of his thievish propensity than if he had had twelve months' imprisonment with hard labour. Very soon after this, he also enlisted for a soldier, deserted, was several times in prison, and ultimately died a raving maniac in Wakefield. Poor F——! thy miserable fate might have similarly closed my own chequered and sinful existence! That God

---

42 Teasdale refers to the story of Haman, main antagonist in the Book of Esther, who instigates a plot to kill the Jews of Ancient Persia. Haman's scheme is foiled by Queen Esther, and he is hanged. The origin of the quotation is unclear: it could be an amalgamation of 'His mischief shall return upon his own head, and his violent dealing shall come down upon his own pate' (Psalms, 7:16) and 'the wicked shall fall by his own wickedness' (Proverbs, 11: 5).

should have thus singled me out from my wicked companions, made me the monument of his boundless mercy, fills me with a deeper loathing of myself, and a more adoring gratitude to my lovely and exalted Saviour, and compels me to exclaim with the venerable poet, Charles Wesley, —

> *What am I, O thou glorious God?*
> *And what my father's house to Thee,*
> *That thou such mercy should'st bestow*
> *On me, the vilest reptile, me?*
> *I take the blessing from above,*
> *And wonder at Thy ceaseless love.*[43]

CHAPTER IV

A new era of a more promising and influential character now took place. Having become closely associated with a number of zealous amateurs from the richer and more aristocratic portions of society, who were attracted by the supposed rising genius of Harvey Teasdale, I took a room on my own account, at the back of the Brown Cow, Lee Croft. I shall not record the wicked scenes that were enacted in this room. I shall not lift the curtain. Would that I could as easily blot them from memory's dark escutcheon; but, alas! in sombre moments they come like dark spectres of the past, conjured up by memory – "busy, meddling memory"[44] – to haunt me with their hideous forms, and it is only by remembering that —

> *There is a fountain filled with blood,*
> *Drawn from Immanuel's veins,*
> *And sinners plunged beneath that flood,*
> *Lose all their guilty stains.*[45]

---

43 Charles Wesley, 'What am I, O thou glorious God!' *Hymns and Sacred Poems,* 1749 (What am I, O thou glorious God!/Or what my father's house to thee/That thou such blessings hast bestowed/On me, the vilest reptile me!/I take the blessings from above,/And wonder at thy causeless love').

44 Probably a reference to 'The Grave' (c.1743), a poem by Robert Blair (1699-1746): 'She drops; whilst busy-meddling memory,/In barbarous succession, musters up/The past endearments of their softer hours,/Tenacious of its theme' (ll. 78-81).

45 William Cowper (1731-1800), 'Praise for the Fountain Opened' (1772),

I can get the relief from torturing rack and burning hell into which they would otherwise throw me. Amongst those who were associated with me to receive instruction in the "buskin" business,[46] was one whom I now see holding a very influential position in the town. He was to have made another "man monkey," to which his high ambition aspired as the very acme of triumphant genius; but, somehow, whether nature had neglected to endow him with that physical flexibility and tenacity of nerve requisite for the task, or whether his genius failed to reach the ideal in which the important character had portrayed itself to his mind, certain it is that he made a most miserable failure of it. But, whilst the devil failed to mould him to his purpose, God has shown in his subsequent history that there was a much nobler position both in the Church and in the world, which he intended him to occupy. He is now an ornament to the town, and a useful member of the Church; being born of the spirit, he is now a new creature in Christ.

I opened another room shortly after this, at Matilda Tavern, Doctors' Fields. One night we were advertised to play "Eugene Aram."[47] A man of the name of Finch, who was recommended as being a first-rate amateur performer, and who himself boasted of his capabilities in the histrionic art, was expected on this occasion to give quite an *éclat*[48] to our performances, when, lo! just at the last moment, his memory completely failed him, and he could not utter a word of his part. There was nothing for it, however, but his performing a dumb show, opening and shutting his lips as though he was speaking, a prompter being behind the scenes uttering

---

published as part of the *Olney Hymns*. ('There is a fountain fill'd with blood/ Drawn from Emmanuel's veins;/And sinners, plung'd beneath that flood,/Lose all their guilty stains').

46 In addition to the contemporary word 'busking' to denote performing on the streets to generate revenue, a 'buskin' also refers to a tragic dramatic piece. Teasdale might be ironically comparing his emergence into theatre with a 'buskin', i.e. his emerging success as man monkey would ultimately end in tragedy.

47 A play based on the life of Eugene Aram (1704-1759), English schoolmaster and infamous murderer. Aram was found guilty of murdering his associate, Daniel Clark, and attempted suicide before he was hanged in 1759. Other texts, inspired by Aram's crimes, were in circulation, such as Thomas Hood's (1799-1845) ballad 'The Dream of Eugene Aram' (c.1829) and Edward Bulwer-Lytton's novel *Eugene Aram* (1832).

48 Brilliance; or a conspicuously successful reputation.

the words. No Sheffield audience could stand this; they first hissed and finally pelted him off the stage, the curtain suddenly falling on his ignoble retreat. Oh, the troubles of a stage manager! An infuriated audience writhing under a sense or fraud and robbery! Oh, for the eloquence of Demosthenes[49] to still the waves of their exasperated ire! The curtain rises again; the man monkey prepares to brunt the storm with a comic song. Shade of Garrick![50] what a falling off was there. But the ruse succeeded, and by a series of recitations and songs we passed the rubicon and closed the performance – not before, however, Mr. Finch begged to retrieve his injured fame by singing a song, which, like his acting, was a signal failure, the audience threatening to give him when he came out a ducking in the horse pond close by, but which, unfortunately, I was destined, without the aid of the audience, to receive in his stead. On coming out of the room, and passing by the side of the dyke a part of the footpath had given way, and I, with my pockets full of copper, and my hands in both pockets to keep down the money, was precipitated into the dyke, and, to crown the misfortune, to save myself I jerked out my hands, which brought out the copper, and so became irredeemably lost in the water.

At a booth, or portable theatre, erected in the Corn Exchange, belonging to a man passing under the quaint patronymic of "old Knock," I was engaged to play the part of "Eugene Aram." It was during the memorable election riots, at the first municipal election after the passing of the Reform Bill, when nine victims, whose deaths are a lasting disgrace to all concerned in that ill-managed affair, were laid out in the Town Hall, awaiting the coroner's inquest. [51] One was a watchman, in the execution of his duty; another was a woman, and another a boy under nine years of age. They were shot at the side of Wiley's, Old No. 12, by the soldiers who were stationed just under the gateway of the old Tontine Inn. After

---

49 Demosthenes (384-322BCE) was a Greek statesman whose eloquent speeches established him as one of the greatest and most powerful orators of Ancient Greece.

50 Probably another reference to famous English actor David Garrick (1717-1779).

51 Teasdale is probably referring to the riots following the Great Reform Act of 1832, the 'first thoroughgoing attempt to redraw the political map and define which categories of persons should, and which should not, have the vote' (Eric J. Evans, *The Great Reform Act of 1832* (London: Routledge, 1994), p. 2).

the performance at the booth, as I was coming home, I happened to have a horse-pistol, which had been doing duty at the booth that night; its voice however, had not been heard, for the very valid reason that it had no lock, and it could not even strike fire. One of the special constables, a man, "big with a little brief authority,"[52] and smelling treason in the very atmosphere, chanced to see my harmless pistol, which appeared to him a very formidable weapon of conspiracy, was seized with a sudden fit of patriotism, and wishing, no doubt, to signalize himself as a very vigilant and valiant officer of the Crown, attempted to arrest me as a rioter. To prove that I was no rioter, I gave him an Irishman's *argumentum ad hominum*,[53] and to escape further annoyance, I took to flight, pursued by half a dozen "specials," and reached home in safety. I cannot, however, dismiss the pistol without relating another ludicrous adventure, fraught with not a little trouble, of which this pistol was the innocent cause. It was during the great Chartist agitation, when the Chartists were showing their zeal for the five points of the Charter by a physical force demonstration, which was attended to show the martial valour of the people in defence of their political rights;[54] but history shews that, in nine cases out of ten, for people to play at soldiering is but the manifestation of insane folly, and is productive only of misery, penury, and woe.

One night a watchman was shot at by a Chartist near to our house; the shot went through his hat, grazed his head, but leaving the man in the partial possession of his senses; he sprung his rattle and followed in

---

52 Teasdale is probably referring to Shakespeare's *Measure for Measure*, 2.2 ('but man, proud man,/ Dress'd in a little brief authority').

53 A fallacious argument that attacks a person's motives or character, rather than their opinions.

54 Chartism was a reform movement in Britain from 1838 to 1848 that sought manhood suffrage, payment of Members of Parliament, equal electoral districts, annual parliaments, voting by ballot, and the abolition of property qualifications for MPs. Sheffield's Paradise Square became the scene of numerous protests and rallies in favour of Chartism, with thousands of people turning up to support the cause. In early 1840, the Sheffield uprising, led by Samuel Holberry, was set to take place. Through looting, threatening, arson, and murder, the aim of the uprising was to frighten those eligible to vote into making the Charter the law of the land. The plot was foiled, however, and those involved captured and tried (John Salt, *Chartism in South Yorkshire* (Sheffield: University of Sheffield Institute of Education, 1971)).

pursuit of the man. The poor watchman, in his bewilderment, fancied that he had seen the man enter our house; he knocked at the door, upon which I got up, put my head out of the window, and asked him what was the matter. The watchman, fancying that I was the man, demanded immediate admittance, which I had no sooner given, than the watchman, turning on his "bullseye,"[55] glanced round the room, and espied this harmless old horse-pistol hung upon a nail, cried out to some more watchman who had just made their appearance at the spring of the rattle, "That is the man, here is the very pistol he has shot me with." Happily for myself, the dilapidated condition of the pistol made it not very difficult for me to prove my innocence, or I might in spite of my protestations, have been taken up, like poor Clarke, a local preacher, and put in the lock-up for the remainder of the night. The guardians of the law have a very summary and not very pleasant way of dealing with suspected persons, and are sometimes very oblivious of the laws of evidence, and instead of acting on the English maxim to consider every man innocent until he is proved to be guilty, they invest the syllogism, and act on its contra.

A clown, of the name of Phillips, came to Sheffield to engage a number of actors for a travelling theatre, which was then stationed at Retford.[56] He offered very liberal terms, in fact, an all but equal share in the profits, without risk, and besides which he gave such a flaming account of its future success that to us, who were but neophytes in the profession, was so attractive and alluring that some of those engaged actually broke up their homes to allow this will-o'-the-wisp phantom of seeking their fortunes out of this vagabondising comedy. One of my companions in this erratic expedition is now, while I am writing this autobiography, passing through the swellings of Jordan,[57] and, apparently, within a few hours of that "bourne from whence no traveller returns."[58] No fears distress him

---

55   In this context, 'bullseye' is a lantern.

56   Retford (Nottinghamshire) is a market town thirty miles south-east of Sheffield.

57   Jeremiah 12:5 ('if in the land of peace, wherein thou trustedst, they wearied thee, then how wilt thou do in the swelling of Jordan?'). The River Jordan spans over 320km through the Sea of Galilee to the Dead Sea. According to Christianity, it is the place Jesus was baptised by John the Baptist.

58   Teasdale is probably referring to Shakespeare's *Hamlet*, 3.1 ('The undiscovered

now; a holy calm settles on his breast and is stamped on his brow; he speaks of Heaven as his assured inheritance; his faith takes hold of the Mediator, and rests on Calvary;[59] hallelujahs of devout gratitude to the Lamb of God are the unceasing utterances of his lips, and give a gleam of heaven-like peace to his countenance, as if, like Christian in "Pilgrim's Progress,"[60] he had looked into the gates of the celestial city and caught a slanting beam from the opened doors.

It was on a cold winter's morning when we started to walk to Retford. Phillips amused us on the road with stories and glowing pictures of that Eldorado[61] towards which we were bending our steps. An actor's life is similar to that of a gambler – a few prizes are mingled with an innumerable number of blanks, very much like an Irishman's raffle. I knew an Irishman who had a piece of cloth which cost him 12s. He put it in a raffle at sixpence each, and sold 400 tickets, by which he cleared £9 8s., there being 399 blanks to one paltry prize; and not very much better is the life of an actor. When we reached Retford we found the booth covered with snow. The owner was a man named Hall, an ex-pugilist, with a bloated countenance that gave us to understand that it would take all our united earnings. And all the golden visions with which Phillips had regaled us on the road, to drown the spark in that man's thirsty throat; and though it was fair week, with performances every night, not one single copper could we get from that drunken sot for all the grimaces outside and all the acting inside that wretched booth. We came, we supposed, to make our fortunes, but instead of embracing, as we hoped, Dame Fortune dressed in her gay, holiday clothes, we found, as many others have done, that there are two ladies in the Fortune family, and that instead of the mother, we had got the daughter – Misfortune, in her most

---

country, from whose bourn/No traveller returns').

59 The Mediator is reference to Christ: 'For there is one God, and one mediator between God and men, the man Christ Jesus' (1 Timothy 2:5). Calvary is the place where Christ was crucified: 'And when they were come to the place, which is called Calvary, there they crucified him, and the malefactors, one on the right hand, and the other on the left' (Luke 23:33).

60 John Bunyan (1628-1688), *The Pilgrim's Progress*, 1678.

61 Originally a fabled city in South America, rich in treasure and sought by Spanish explorers, that has come to symbolise any place of great riches and opportunity; Teasdale uses Eldorado to express his monetary wants.

beggarly garb. I need say no more to describe our wretched position than the fact that I had to live on russet boots, cotton tights, combat swords, leather belts, daggers, &c, – that is to say, I sold them to buy food; and when these were done, we had nothing for it but to return home, poorer if not wiser men.

It was not long after this that I was induced to accept another brilliant engagement, under the management of Alfred Finch, who possessed a portable theatre, stationed at Conisbro',[62] intending to give a treat to the inhabitants of that rustic and exceedingly neat little village, possessing the far-famed ruin of her castle and keep, which Sir Walter Scott has immortalised in its very exciting romance of "Ivanhoe."[63] I say it was intended to give these villagers a treat in the ever-attractive wonders of the drama, but whether we had miscalculated and over-estimated our powers of attraction, or these inhabitants of sylvan[64] life were too prosaic and unimaginative in their mental constitution to appreciate the immortal bard, or too poor to pay for the luxury, certain it is that the straits of poverty began to tell seriously upon our condition. Nor were we alone in the vale of poverty. A rival theatre, under the noted proprietorship of Dan Kemp, had come to share the favours of these rustic swains. To make known to the scattered inhabitants the glories of our establishment, our music (for what is a theatre without it?) consisted of a big drum, certainly of marvellous sonorous power, but alas! it lacked variety in its tones; and here our rival, Dan Kemp, had a great advantage over us, for one of Dan's actors had married a German lady, who happened to possess a splendid hurdy-gurdy. It was certainly mortifying to be outdone in this respect; but there was one consolation – we could and did drown the effect with the higher notes of our big drum. But neither the hurdy-gurdy nor the big drum could draw the coppers out of the empty pockets of these country bumpkins. In our vexation, and prompted by our needs, we laid contributions on their gardens, in the matter of potatoes and cabbages, which helped to stifle the cravings of hunger that became exceedingly urgent from the protracted fast which our non-success had occasioned.

---

62   Conisbrough (Yorkshire) is a town thirteen miles north-east of Sheffield.

63   Walter Scott (1771-1832) published *Ivanhoe* in 1820.

64   Isolated communities living in attractive countryside. Teasdale uses the phrase to emphasise the simplistic, uncultured nature of the area's inhabitants and their lack of appreciation for his performance.

A circumstance occurred here which, though small in itself, is not without its moral as illustrative of that particular providence which is as manifest in supplying the wants of the poorest child of destitution and of want as in directing the mighty affairs of empires and of worlds. In this village of Conisbro' lived a Mr. Carswell, who had formerly been a neighbour of my father's. This man, or rather his wife, had become acquainted with my destitute condition, and sent for me to give me something to eat, and, with a motherly feeling, recommended me to go home, not forgetting to give me sixpence, as she said to help me on the road.

It might be thought that these repeated failures would have so subdued the ardour of my profession that I should have given it up for the sure gains of my proper calling as a cutler. But the ruling passion was too strong for any wave of disappointment, however great, completely to destroy. Very soon after this, I opened the old room at the Black Beer Brewery, and engaged a number of "stars," whose far-famed abilities promised soon to retrieve my fallen fortunes. One of these "stars" was named Graham, who, when I engaged him told me, with an actor's ready bounce, that I should find it to be the greatest hit of the season, which was speedily verified, but not very pleasantly to him, at least, for they hooted and so hit him with pop bottles, &c., that I was obliged suddenly to let fall the curtain, which as he was making a not very dignified exit, hit him so severely that he roared again with pain, and the audience, in a fit of uncontrollable laughter, cried out, "Encore – encore – encore!" I was ready enough to repeat my part of the performance, but Graham, satisfied with the impression so strongly realised, refused the benefit which the audience were prepared so abundantly to bestow. This closed the season of the Black Beer Brewery Theatre.

The Adelphi Theatre,[65] now called the Alexandra Opera House, was built about this time, and was opened by a person called Ryan (not the celebrated Dick Ryan) with a first-class double company. That "the race is

---

65 The Adelphi Theatre was built in 1837. According to Bryen D. Hillerby's *The Lost Theatres of Sheffield* (Wharncliffe Books, 1999), pp. 34-8, the Adelphi 'was reputedly a faithful copy of Astley's famous amphitheatre in Westminster' and was originally known as 'The Circus'. In 1865, the theatre was purchased by Thomas Youdan who renamed it the Alexandra Theatre and Opera House. It was demolished in the early twentieth century.

not to the swift, nor the battle to the strong,"[66] is a truth as applicable to theatrical management as to anything else; and thus the Adelphi, whilst prospering under a pseudo-philanthropist and ex-Town Councillor, ruined poor Ryan. It was then closed for a short period, after which, being assisted by some friends, I opened it for dramatic performances, commencing with a piece entitled "The Factory Strike." The house was full – crowded, for which I was so grateful that I gave an extra piece, so that it was one o'clock before the performance closed. However, the audience was well satisfied, and I was considerably in pocket. An actor of very considerable promise and ability, whose name was Edwin Huggins,[67] or Edwin, as he was more popularly known by, came from London, where he had been "starring" with considerable *éclat*, to whom, for a certain pecuniary consideration, I let the Adelphi. Edwin was another victim of that curse of all civilised life – drink. He might have made a fortune in his profession. He was spoken of very highly on his first introduction to the London boards in the critique of the day. This so elated him that he must needs celebrate it in the courts of Bacchus, and the consequence was that, on the third night of his metropolitan career, he was so drunk that the manager summarily dismissed him; and so, like a   fallen star, he came down to the provinces to attempt, with the partial halo of two nights' Drury Lane display, to gain popularity in minor provincial towns. But, alas! he brought with him his besetting sin, and that poverty which is necessarily associated with it. To gratify his propensity, he used to levy contributions on all who would, as he said, "kindly lend him a trifle, only for a short time, to make up the sum that he was, unfortunately, just then in need of." I was aware of this habit of Edwin's, and cautioned those whom I thought might be made his victims. Among the band whom Edwin had engaged was Reuben Hallam, author of "Wadsley Jack."[68] At the morning rehearsal, Edwin took Reuben Hallam on one side, asking

---

66 Ecclesiastes 9:11.

67 Possibly a reference to Benjamin Edwin Huggins (1798-1873). The scanty information available states that Huggins was a comedy actor, known as 'Mr Edwin', who took several lead roles in Drury Lane. He married in 1818 at Sheffield cathedral.

68 Reuben Hallam (1818-1908), also known as Wadsley Jack, was the author of the autobiographical work *Wadsley Jack; or, the Humours and Adventures of a Travelling Cutler* (1866). Hallam was a cutler, author, and musician.

the particular favour of having a few minutes' conversation on private and confidential business. Reuben, however, was quite awake to this peculiarity of his quondam[69] friend, and was framing in his own mind the excuse for that want of sympathy with poor Edwin which his refusal to help would seem to imply.

So intent, however, were each upon the real farce that was then performing on the tragic boards, that neither of them perceived an open trap-door that lay direct in their path, and so they suddenly disappeared in the in the dark abyss, from which they as suddenly re-appeared, not a little begrimed, but happily without injury, excepting poor Reuben, who, unfortunately, had taken him with his fiddle, which was shattered to pieces. Edwin, with his usual professed generosity, declared he would replace it with a new one, but Reuben knew the value of his promises, and refused to be comforted therewith. In the evening before the performances commenced, Edwin called all the company together, informing us with great pomposity that, as it was absolutely certain that the house would be filled to overflowing (he expected there would be a great rush at the doors), he begged that we would kindly assist him in taking the tickets, and see that no one came in without paying. I had, however, just been on the balcony outside the theatre, and knew that there was not a single person waiting, and it was then the time for opening. However, just as Edwin had appointed each his position, a loud knocking was heard at the doors. "Now gentlemen," cried Edwin, "to you posts, they're coming! Open the gallery doors first, and let in the gods." It was done, when in rolls a sweep, who cried out, "'Twas me that knocked – I have brought the bill-board, and you said you would give me sixpence for my trouble." He was allowed to go into the gallery as compensation for his work. When the time came for the performance to begin, there was not a soul in the house but the sweep. I went round with two more to the stage door, and found several boys, who offered us two-pence if we would let them in. We did so, and set off to spend the money. Poor Edwin, in desperation at his loss, discovered these lads, and in his fury scattered them in all directions.

Alfred Raynor, who at the time I am writing, holds a prominent position on the London boards, made his first appearance as an amateur at the Adelphi.   He played with myself in a piece called "The Trial by

---

69 'former'.

Battle,"[70] in which two youths, one the hero, the other a ruffian, stamped with crimes of the deepest dye, is doomed to fall by the sword of the hero, as a proof that sooner or later, virtue is sure to be rewarded, and crime to receive its just punishment. I played the part of the hero, and Raynor that of the ruffian. But whether Raynor did not thoroughly understand the plot, and the part he had to play, or whether his pride rebelled at the indignity of being beaten, certain it is that I could not prevail on him to fall. Round the stage we went, clash went the swords, repeatedly I called upon him to fall, until, vexed at his obstinacy, what was only a sham fight at the commencement, became a real fight at the close, for tripping up his heels I brought him on his back, amidst thunders of applause, during which the curtain fell – the ruffian prostrate, the hero pointing his sword in triumph over his prostrate form.

Sometime after this I was engaged manager for Milner's Concert Room, where we played short pieces interspersed with songs. One of our best singers was a man named Grimes, a joiner, who came from Stockport; he was a very good hand at his trade, and could earn good wages, but preferred singing and idleness, with a very precarious living, to settled employment and certain wages. This man sported a diamond ring, of which he was not a little vain; but one evening he happened to leave the ring on the dressing-table in his bed-room. When he got to the Concert Room he discovered his loss and immediately returned for the ring. When, lo! it was not to be found. A fellow lodger was the only person in the house when he left, and he at once charged him with the theft. The man indignantly denied it, and proceeded to call upon God to strike him dead if he had got it. I have no doubt that many such impious appeals have been made to God's omniscience without His deigning to answer them with the thunderbolt of His wrath, but there are times when the appeal is not made in vain, and this was one – he died instantly, and the ring was found in his pocket. Never, perhaps, was crime more quickly followed by detection and punishment, and never more signal proof afforded of the existence of that awful God that "searcheth the hearts and trieth the reins of the children of men."[71] These awful illustrations of

---

70   A play published in 1818 by William Barrymore (1759-1830). Its full title is *Trial by Battle; Or Heaven Defend the Right*.

71   An interpretation of Psalms 7:9 ('Oh let the wickedness of the wicked come to an end; but establish the just: for the righteous God trieth the hearts and

God's righteous judgment shall not be in vain. That they are not more influential in producing conviction upon men's minds is but another proof of the truth of the Saviour's declaration, that "If they believe not in Moses and the Prophets, neither will they be persuaded, though one rose from the dead."[72]

One great difficulty which we have to contend with in all amateur theatricals is the tricks and freaks which memory will sometimes play with some of the young hands, which is the cause of very great annoyance to those who have the management of such exhibitions; hence the necessity of rehearsals, to see that everyone is perfect in their parts. I remember one very good actor as an amateur; he was the most fluent and ready at rehearsals, I felt proud of having to present for the first time so promising a "star." In the evening, when his part had to come, with a proud step he went on to the stage, took up his position, and stood, mouth open, but without being able to utter a single word; his memory failed him in his hour of need. The audience have no pity on these unfortunate offenders, so they hissed and hooted till the curtain dropped; and he, poor wight, took to flight, and jumped out of a window which looked into the back yard. But, alas! his misfortunes did not end here, for in jumping out of the window he jumped into a water-butt that was underneath the window, and, but for help, might have made a more serious exit than from the mimic stage.

Milner gave up his concert room and bought a portable theatre, and gave me an engagement as clown; this brought me out more fully in that new character as "man monkey", for which I have, since that time, been mainly distinguished. Our first engagement was in Halifax. We built our theatre in Northgate, and the first night it was so crowded that the gallery broke down, creating such a scene of confusion, broken limbs, torn garments, and screams of agony, which I hope never to witness again. Not long after, the booth, during a storm of wind and hail, was shattered to pieces. Elijah Charles, a bookbinder (whom some of my readers will know), and I purchased the *débris,* and rebuilt it, intending to start for ourselves as travelling comedians. At first our receipts were next to *nil,* but at the Sheffield Fair we made a successful hit, which made up for past

reins').

72 Luke 16:31 ('If they hear not Moses and the prophets, neither will they be persuaded, though one rose from the dead').

failures. But these gains were quickly spent, and my partner, Charles, being a *thirsty soul*, we had to sell the booth, and so dissolved partnership. I think it is Gough who says, "How much of intellect, genius, and mental power is swallowed up in rum or alcohol."[73] What a host have I not seen of spirits, illuminated with the brightest rays of genius – men whose talent would have fitted for, and enabled them to shine in any station of life, but who, having imbibed the fatal cup, have been dashed from the pedestal of fame to the darkest shades of sottishness, so loathsome and degraded that the lowest savagery of heathenism might shrink from its touch. These men never intended to have descended thus. Could the future have been pictured to them, they would indignantly have replied, like one of old, "Is thy servant a dog that he should do this thing?"[74] The insidious element of this cup of intoxication, and the almost incredible number of its victims, the utter wreck by hell and remorse to which they are doomed, should make each man and woman forswear the inebriating potion, and seek, in the total abstinence pledge, the only security from the inevitable vortex. Dear reader, let me beseech you to enter this peaceful harbour of total abstinence from all intoxicating drinks; you will at once become the possessor of a peace that surpasseth every other,[75] except that of the Gospel, and will insure to you, while you keep it, an infallible security from the fearful doom of the drunkard.

Dick Ryan, whose name in connection with a travelling theatre is known in almost every village in the kingdom, came to Sheffield, with whom I made an engagement as clown in his not very renowned or elegant company. I may state here, without any great display of egotism, that I was the "star" of the establishment, and added not a little to Dick's varying funds. Amongst the persons composing Ryan's travelling group was an eccentric character named Joe Smith, whose chief foible was his aping of gentility; his strut, his cocked hat, his sequential air, staggering

---

73   Teasdale is probably referring to John B. Gough (1817-1886), a United States Temperance orator whose *An Autobiography* (1845) details his conversion from alcoholism to sobriety, the template Teasdale also uses.

74   2 Kings 8:13 ('is thy servant a dog, that he should do this great thing?').

75   Probably an interpretation of Philippians 4:7 ('And the peace of God, which passeth all understanding, shall keep your hearts and minds through Christ Jesus').

gait, and the big words with which he tried to "astonish the natives,"[76] made him a very conspicuous appendage, even to Ryan's strangely assorted company. Some of the actors called one day at Joe's lodgings, and wanted him to go with them. Joe was rather in *déshabille*,[77] and called to his wife, who was upstairs, to bring down his coat – his No. 3 best. His wife, not aware that company had come in, shouted out, "Tha knows that tha's only one coat, an' it's i't'wesh tub!"[78] Poor Joe! It was a terrible blow to his pride thus to be exposed to those who were very likely never to let him hear the last of it.

Ryan took the Adelphi, and when my benefit came on, I hit upon a very novel expedient to draw a full house, and it succeeded admirably. I advertised, in flaming placards, that I would sail down the river in a washing-tub drawn by ducks. This startling announcement took Sheffield by surprise, and drew my fellow-townsmen by thousands to witness this marvellous and unprecedented sight. It was computed that there were not less than seventy thousand persons to view this aquatic show. It was not without danger, however as the sequel proved, for just as I got opposite Cocker's Wire Works, the force of the crowd was so strong, that a wall, covered with people, fell into the water. The piercing shrieks that accompanied the fall might have appalled a stouter heart than mine, and made a sensation not easily shaken off. I remember seeing a pair of crutches appear above the water, and then going down, and an old woman rising, whose ghastly features were made more hideous by the way she screamed for help, and cursed old Harvey and his ducks. Thank God there were no lives lost. There was a similar feat enacted at Yarmouth, and one hundred lives were lost. A thrilling incident is related concerning that awful calamity. An iron bridge that spanned the river was so crowded with people that it broke, and hundreds were precipitated into the river. Amongst them was a young man, a powerful swimmer, who was compelled to strike off many of the drowning creatures who clung to him for rescue; but one beautiful young lady so tenaciously grasped hold of him that he could not shake her off. The young man seemed to feel that he must in some way release himself from her grasp, or they must both

---

76 A phrase that seems to crop up a lot in early nineteenth-century writing, but its origin or explicit meaning are uncertain.

77 Being partially or carelessly dressed.

78 'You know you've only got one coat, and it's in the wash tub!'.

perish; he instantly drew from his breast coat pocket a clasp knife, and plunged it into her heart.[79] With an unearthly shriek, she sank to rise no more. It is not likely that the authorities will ever permit the repetition of a scene so fraught with peril. That night the Adelphi was filled from floor to ceiling; it took a large clothes-box to hold my share of the proceeds. I was not a little elated with the success of that day's exploit; but there was a "fly in the ointment,"[80] for just as my wife and myself were proceeding up King Street, carrying the heavy box of treasure, the bottom fell out, and all the coppers rolled into the street. Here was a pretty mess. It required all my efforts to keep the people off while my wife picked up the money – at least, what she could find, and what was not stolen, for, in spite of all I could do, some of it they would and did have.

I now commenced, keeping a public-house, called not appropriately, "The Clown's Head," for never was there folly so hideously and wickedly portrayed as in the scenes that were nightly enacted in that cauldron of insanity, vice, and folly. From this den I went to another in Paradise Square, where every crime, I blush to tell, was enacted, save that of murder, if that, indeed, might be excepted, where a man was left for dead, with his skull beaten in with a poker. And these are everyday occurrences, so common, that except in cases of more than ordinary atrocity, which demons only might be thought to perpetrate, cease to excite attention, and are done under the sanction and license of a government professedly Christian. What greater proof could be given of the truth of that fearful declaration of that good Old Book, that the Devil is the prince of this

79   The following account is taken from the *Yarmouth Notes 1830-1872* by Frederick Danby Palmer, published in 1889, and was itself a transcription of a contemporary newspaper report on the 'Great Yarmouth Suspension Bridge Disaster' of 1845: 'Nelson, the Clown at Mr. Cooke's Circus, had undertaken to swim in a tub, drawn by four geese … a foolish exhibition – but it was one which, from its novelty in Yarmouth, was calculated to attract the multitude … Already had he reached Bessey's Wharf, not far from the Bridge, when one or two of the rods were observed to give way … The chains broke, and as quick as the passing thought, one entire side fell, and the whole mass of the human beings, whose numbers were estimated from three to four hundred, were swept into the river below'.

80   An idiom most likely derived from Ecclesiastes 10:1 ('Dead flies cause the ointment of the apothecary to send forth a stinking savour: so doth a little folly him that is in reputation for wisdom and honour').

world. Oh! when will He come whose right it is to reign? and whose coming will be the signal for the binding of that old serpent, the Devil, that he shall deceive the nations no more.

I left this house to make my first appearance in London, and for six or seven weeks performed low comedy at Astley's Amphitheatre,[81] but having had a quarrel with the stage manager, I withdrew from the engagement. I again joined Dick Ryan, who was then playing in Grantham Theatre. It was in this theatre that the most daring feat that ever was performed in any theatre took place. The times were dull, the drama was getting stale, and it required something out of the common line to bring the people into the theatre, and their money into the manager's pocket. It was announced that the man monkey would make the daring and unparalleled leap from the gallery to the stage! Surely this was excitement enough, even in this sensational age, to bring crowds of thoughtless pleasure-seekers to gaze in wonder on the tragic leap. I need hardly say it was a splendid and great financial success.

Thomas B. Lacy[82] opened the Theatre Royal, Sheffield,[83] and I was engaged to act as pantaloon[84] in the pantomime that was then performing. G. L. Saunders, Esq.,[85] late Chairman of the Sheffield Board of

---

81 Astley's Amphitheatre was a performance venue in London, opened in 1773 by Philip Astley (1742-1814). It is regarded as the first modern circus.

82 It is possible Teasdale is referring to Thomas Hailes Lacy (1809-1873), an actor, theatrical publisher, and dramatist who became the manager of Sheffield's Theatre Royal in 1841.

83 According to Hillerby's *The Lost Theatres of Sheffield* (pp. 111-25), the Theatre Royal opened in 1778. It was closed for five weeks in 1901 for renovation, only to be destroyed by fire in December 1935.

84 In a Harlequinade, the Pantaloon was often an absurd old man, who was the butt of jokes, and would ultimately be outwitted by the Harlequin.

85 The *Hudson Collection of Early Playbills* (University of Sheffield Library: Special Collections and Archives, Ref: PE 17) has a George Saunders listed as an actor who travelled the world, gaining 'notable reviews for his acting throughout his career ... He owned a Music and Stationery Saloon on the High Street in Sheffield, whilst performing duties to the Theatre Royal in the city.'

Guardians,[86] was the harlequin;[87] and I may say here that a better horn-pipe dancer than G. L. Saunders, Esq., never appeared on the stage of the Theatre Royal. Two clowns were announced with a "great flourish of trumpets,"[88] but they made a miserable failure of it, and were hissed off the stage, and thus it devolved upon me to play both clown and pantaloon. The harlequin had to leap through a picture in one scene, and he thought to have it all to himself, for no one was supposed capable of following him in so agile a spring. But the man who had leaped from the gallery to the stage was not to be outdone by even the best harlequin in the world, so I followed, leaping through like a dart, bringing down thunders of applause – not a little to the chagrin of the mortified harlequin.

The play of "Jack Sheppard"[89] now made its first appearance, and became a great favourite, especially with the lower orders. I took a part in it, and it suggested itself to my mind that it would be a good thing to open the Adelphi with. I accordingly opened the Adelphi, and took the leading character of Jack Shepherd, the Highwayman, and realised a considerable sum by the undertaking. Soon after this, Alfred Raynor and I joined Douglas's travelling theatre – a splendid affair of its kind. Raynor took the leading characters, and I the clown and man monkey. Raynor became a great favourite with the people, and thus managed to make good receipts. At Macclesfield Fair we came in contact with a rival theatre, but without boasting, I think I may say that we eclipsed anything they could do, and they were obliged to make a hasty retreat, leaving us sole masters of the fair ground. It was here that I had an encounter

---

86 The Board of Guardians referred to here is part of an *ad hoc* network of authorities that administered the Poor Law in the United Kingdom between 1835-1930.

87 In a Harlequinade the Harlequin was the romantic male lead, a high spirited, funny, and foppish character who won the affections of Columbine.

88 Teasdale is probably referring to Shakespeare's *Henry VIII*, 4.1 ('A lively flourish of trumpets').

89 Teasdale is probably referring to a play c.1839 by John Baldwin Buckstone (1802-1879) based on the life of Cockney thief, Jack Sheppard (1702-1724). Sheppard notoriously escaped from prison four times before his final capture in 1724. He was then convicted and hanged. During his final stay in prison, visitors could pay to view Sheppard, bound in iron chains. Over 200,000 people attended his execution. His life and death inspired many works of art and fiction.

with some navvies,[90] that brought out all the pugilistic powers for which I had been famous in my youth. It was on the morning of our last day in Macclesfield that Raynor and myself were in a taproom of a public-house, when there came in three rough navvies, followed soon after by a girl playing a hurdy-gurdy. The navvies began taking indecent liber-ties with the girl, who, being good looking, and apparently modest in her deportment, roused fiercely within me a spirit of gallantry, and I boldly rebuked the licentious brutes. They, in their turn, relying on their numerical superiority, began to physically attack me. Thus it became a struggle between rough brute force on the one hand, and agility, nerve, and pugilistic tactics on the other. I did not come off quite scatheless, but I gave my adversaries such a pummelling that they swore vengeance against the man monkey, and went to their gang to get a reinforcement to their numbers for an attack at night. They waited outside the theatre for my coming out at the close of the performance; but, aware of their design, I made my exit through the canvas at the back, and so escaped my antagonists, which greatly increased their ire at being thus so successfully outwitted, but they swore yet to have their revenge.

The next day we removed to Stockport, where we had a long and profitable season. The play of "The Green Bushes"[91] came out, which necessitated the lengthening of the stage floor. The theatre was built in what is called the Castle Yard, and this new portion of the stage came right on to the wall at the back. This wall stood a great height above the houses in the street below, and, from some cause or other, it gave way, and brought part of the stage along with it into the street. Had it not oc-curred far in the night, when we had all left, the consequences might have been serious and fatal. A very ludicrous incident occurred during our stay here, which I may relate as showing the truth of Byron's quaint remark, that "there is but one step from the sublime to the ridiculous."[92] One night we were playing "Hamlet." I was the Gravedigger, and in the scene

---

90 'Navvies', or Navigators, were manual labourers on a building site or excavation.

91 A reference to John Baldwin Buckstone's 1845 play *The Green Bushes; Or, a Hundred Years Ago*.

92 Teasdale appears to have made an error. This quote is in fact widely attrib-uted to Napoleon upon his retreat from Russia in 1812, as recorded in Abbé de Pradt's *Histoire de l'ambassade dans le grand duché de Varsovie en 1812* (1815).

where the gravedigger is in the grave pursuing his employment and singing snatches of songs, with Hamlet on stage at the time, a quarrel ensued
between Hamlet and the Gravedigger, the rights of which I cannot now
remember, but the consequence was that Hamlet and the Gravedigger
had a regular set-to, which was the source of great amusement to the
audience, and summarily closed the very unique evening's entertainment.

I now left this establishment, and joined Thorne's Theatre, at
Darlington, and succeeded greatly as the man monkey. It was here that in
a sword combat I received a stroke across the bridge of my nose that has
left a scar that I shall carry with me to the grave. One night I was playing
the monkey, and when running on a rope right across the theatre, I got
about the middle, when the rope, which was a new one, suddenly gave
a crack, and the audience, thinking it was going to break, and expecting
to see me fall, gave vent to a scream which gave intensity to the interest
of the scene; but I as oblivious of the effect as if nothing was the matter,
finished the feat amidst the most enthusiastic cheering of my admiring
patrons. It was at Darlington the question was raised whether, after all, I
was not a real monkey; and as Englishmen have to decide everything by a
bet, a wager was laid – of course, in a public-house – and I was sent for to
decide, by ocular demonstration whether I was really a man or a monkey.

Our next place was Sunderland, and here we came in contact with
two other rival establishments – Arthur Nelson's[93] and Billy Purvis's [94]
but the monkey took the lead, which caused a conspiracy to spring up
against our establishment by the other two. A procession was formed by
our opponents, with the intention of passing our front, and so taking
along with them the crowd that were gathered before us. I saw through
this manoeuvre, and sought for a counterpoise, and was not long before
I found, not only a check to the manoeuvre, but a revenge for the intended injury, and a cause of deep mortification to both our foes. A lame
old man had entered our theatre, leaving a donkey tied outside. I saw
the procession coming on, preceded and followed by a band of music.
Thorne, our Governor, had been below, and coming on the stage at that

---

93   Probably the aforementioned Arthur Nelson (c.1816-1860), the man responsible for the Great Yarmouth Suspension Bridge Disaster of 1845.

94   Teasdale is probably referring to Billy Purvis (1784-1853), 'renowned
performer' and 'grand old clown', according to *The Life of Billy Purvis, The
Extraordinary, Witty, and Comical Showman* (S. Cowan & Co, 1875) p. 1.

moment, took the whole thing in at once, and became alarmed for the consequences. "Harvey," said he "mind they don't take all our people with them." "All right," said I, "wait a moment. Now then!" I cried, and jumped off the stage, and went to the donkey, got some of the bystanders to help me, lifted the donkey on to the stage, gambolled and grimaced so successfully that the people were perfectly enchanted and entranced, and set up roars of laughter, until the procession had passed, leaving all behind them, not even taking half-a-dozen with them. It was a great success, and I thought old Thorne would have embraced me in the exuberance of his grateful joy.

From this place I made an engagement to play at the Queen's Theatre,[95] Manchester, as clown and monkey and it was acknowledged, by undisputed authority, that mine was the best representation of the monkey tribe that had ever appeared on the stage. It was at the Queen's that I was first dubbed with a German title – "Herr Teasdale" – which stuck to me throughout my theatrical career. From hence my fame began to spread, and I received many offers, and made my selection according to circumstances and salary. In Carlisle, for six nights, immense crowds came to witness the exploits of the man monkey, whose tremendous leaps from the gallery to pit or stage seemed to inspire the silly crowds with a kind of monkey mania. From Carlisle I went to Liverpool, with the same result, and was invited to visit Edinburgh, being engaged to perform there; but, having to pass through Carlisle, I was persuaded to stop and play six nights more, to counteract the attraction of the Circus, which had opened since I left; Mr. Daly, the manager, promising to make all right with the manager at Edinburgh for my non-appearance. I had two engagements at Edinburgh, and it was during the second that appeared at the same time with the far-famed Bosjesmen.[96] They were to give an

---

95 The Queen's Theatre was built on the site of Manchester's Theatre Royal which was destroyed by fire in 1789. The exterior walls mostly survived the fire, however, and the Theatre was rebuilt internally, and altered externally, and reopened under the name of the New Theatre Royal in 1791. The theatre ran under this name until 1809 when it was renamed the New Amphitheatre, and then later the Queen's Theatre. The Theatre closed in March 1869 having been sold at auction. It was demolished shortly afterwards.

96 An interpretation of the Afrikaans word 'boschjesman', meaning 'bushman'. Teasdale is referring to members of a hunter-gatherer community from Southern Africa, specifically the Kalahari region.

entertainment between the pieces. My monkey part was to be the last of the evening's performances. As I was waiting my turn, dressed in my monkey's costume, it being winter, and the weather very severe, I felt exceedingly cold, and got tired of waiting. The audience, too, were tired, I saw, with the Bosjesmen, and anxious for the monkey piece to begin; nor was I mistaken, for they presently began to hiss the African curiosities, so I said to the manager of the Bosjesmen, "I've a good mind to go on and stir them up." He said: "I wish you would." "Well," I said, "get their bows, arrows, and javelins from them and I will go on." He did so, and no sooner was it done than I made my appearance as monkey amongst these – I was going to say fellow-animals, for they were more like animals than men; but, oh dear! what a scene – how shall I describe it? They gave one look from those glittering eyes, and then they flew like lightning in all directions, some over the orchestra into the pit. They were all but frightened to death. The audience thought it was part of the performance, and applauded the scene to the very utmost, their applause continuing long after the curtain had fallen. The next night there was an encore called for, and when the manager went to take from them their implements, you should have seen the dismay of these poor heathens; they expected what was to follow, nor were they mistaken. The audience were in ecstasies at the contortions and antics which my appearance produced; I got between their legs, chucked them up like shuttlecocks, producing a scene too intensely ridiculous to be accurately described.

I had now a long run of successful engagements, and opened, on my own account, the following theatres – Oswestry, Derby, Lincoln, Great Grimsby, Oldham, Halifax, Huddersfield, Burlington, Driffield, St. Helens, Edinburgh, &c., &c. It may be asked by some why I did not make my fortune. With such success as I received, the large sums of money I was paid for a few nights' performances, benefit nights, in which half the proceeds became my share of the gains, ought, you think, to have enabled me to become at least a small capitalist. And so it might, had I had the moral principle of self-denial – had I not been cursed with that appetite for strong drink, which made me careless of consequences, reckless and inexperienced in my speculations. It will be seen that with a bag so full of holes there was no prospect of saving – that riches endless would leave me poor as winter. He that so expends his wealth will in the end be poor indeed.[97]

I received an engagement at Hull, at Mr. Eglinton's Queen's Theatre. They had been playing a pantomime, but it proved a failure. I re-produced it with a few new tricks, introducing my monkey piece, and restored the fallen fortunes of the house. During my engagement, Mr. Eglinton resigned the management to Mr. C. Dillon[98], who, after the run of the pantomime, produced a burlesque called "Fortunio; or, the Seven Gifted Servants." In this piece I came out in a new character from the animal kingdom, one of the amphibious class, viz., a crocodile. My experience, however, in this new class of subjects did not impress me very favourably with its merits; true, it was greatly applauded, but, if it had not succeeded, mine would have been but crocodile tears for its doom.

CHAPTER V

I left Hull and came to Sheffield, took a public house called "The Woodman," in Edward Street, but, not succeeding to my satisfaction, I left it, and went to Liverpool to play clown at the Adelphi. Success followed, but only to steep me still further in guilt and drunkenness. It has often astonished even myself how when in a complete state of inebriation, I have gone through my part without a single bungle, taking those fearful leaps without a single mishap, amidst the plaudits of an admiring public. To show that I am not over-estimating the popularity I obtained in my profession, I have only to say that when my benefit came on, it required two nights to take in the crowds that besieged the theatre for admittance. At the end of the pantomime season I returned to Sheffield, with a new idea, and a grand speculation in a fresh line of business. I was going to realize a fabulous sum by speculating in the provision line.

---

97 Teasdale is probably echoing Luke 18:24-5 ('How hardly shall they that have riches enter into the kingdom of God! For it is easier for a camel to go through a needle's eye, than for a rich man to enter into the kingdom of God').

98 According to the *Hudson Collection of Early Sheffield Playbills*, Charles Dillon (1819-1881) 'gained widespread attention for his role of Hamlet at the City Theatre in London, he began to tour across the country's theatres. In this time, he took management posts at Wolverhampton, Sheffield and Drury Lane, London. He left England to tour the world with his wife, Clara in 1860, continuing to act up until his death' (p. 179)

I bought a large quantity of foreign cheese, hams, and bacon. I took a shop in Queen Street. Need I say what the result was? Have not some of my senior readers shaken their wise heads, not in doubt, but with the absolute certainty of its entire failure? And so it was. I have learnt, in this and similar speculations, that it is absolute folly for a man to expect to prosper in a business in which he has had no experience, and for which Providence may have given him no qualification, and never intended him to enter upon: and thus to go against Providence is to go against destiny, and this is to court a ruin which is sure to follow.

I next took the East Parade Hotel, opposite the Boys' Charity School, and here I prospered, doing the devil's work in the devil's own house, with a concoction or distillation so peculiarly adapted to accomplish the devil's design of turning man's paradise into a hell of misery, that one would almost think it was the creation of the most diabolical inspiration. In this East Parade Hotel we held a judge and jury[99] every Sunday evening. What but the utmost profanity could have prompted so infamous a desecration of God's holy day? How little do Christians know what scenes of wickedness are being perpetrated in the very next building to that in which they are worshipping the Most High. I removed from East Parade to the Norfolk Hotel in Barker Pool, where I was selling, on an average, ten barrels of ale, thirty-six gallons each, per week. Here I tried the Youdan Dodge,[100] and it answered very well. I announced, with a

---

99 The *OED* describes 'judge-and-jury' as a verb used to express trying an individual and passing sentence. In an informal setting, such as a public house, Teasdale might have set up a court room scenario as a form of entertainment, though his exact meaning is unclear.

100 Thomas Youdan (1816-1876) was a beerhouse keeper, music hall manager, and later, successful Sheffield theatre manager. In 1863, after numerous attempts at obtaining a dramatic license that would enable him to turn his Surrey Music Hall into a theatre, he succeeded, but not without opposition; according to Kathleen Barker's *Early Sheffield Music Halls,* Youdan 'flouted the law so flagrantly he was continually being taken to court by either the Theatre Royal proprietors or the current Adelphi manager, or both ... the exasperated magistrates sentenced him to seven days' imprisonment. This blew up into a positive *cause célèbre* with letters to the press, public meetings, and finally, in April 1858, a free pardon from the Queen' (p. 9). When five people died during a performance at the Surrey, Barker comments that it 'says a good deal for the popular faith in Youdan that he was able to reopen within a week, and fill the hall again' (p. 10). Throughout his career, Youdan performed various stunts to earn him popularity

special flourish of trumpets, that I would give soup away every Thursday, to poor people. What disinterested charity was this. First helping to make people poor by making myself rich at their expense, and then dealing out a little soup to make myself famous for a charity I never felt.

I was about this time engaged by Mr. Dillon,[101] at the Theatre Royal, to get up the pantomime of "Queen Mab,"[102] for which he gave me £16 per week, and half clear benefit – that is, half the money taken at the benefit night. We had a crowded house on the night of the benefit; hundreds were unable to gain admittance. Does my reader want to know what I did with the money? I will tell him; and this will illustrate that weakness and failing that showed but too plainly that I was not fit to be entrusted with the possession of wealth. I bought a splendid "turn out," with two ponies and brand new harness. I bought a splendid new dog cart, a coal cart, a large brewer's dray, for which I went into the market to buy a large horse to draw. I saw one in the possession of a dealer that seemed just the one to suit me. The dealer made the horse to go through its paces quite smart. He told me that I had never had such a bargain in my life – and that was true. It was my father over again with the Pea Croft butcher, only with this striking difference: I was sober, while my poor father was drunk, which you will say was in my father's favour, for if he had been sober he would not have done it. I bought the horse, took it home, and when I got to the dram shop door he took it into his head to have a frolic, letting fly with all fours. The people flew in all directions, thinking the horse was mad, and I believe he was. We managed somehow to get him into the stable, where he dropped down, and I could never get him to rise again, so I sold him to John Young, of Pond Lane, for ten shillings. Young

often masked as acts of generosity, such as ordering a four-ton cake containing medals, 'and those who bought a slice of cake containing a medal would be presented with a money gift' (p. 7). Youdan's popularity and generosity seemed to help him circumvent the law on numerous occasions, and Teasdale uses 'Youdan dodge' as an idiom denoting an occasion of his own similar success.

101   Probably a reference to the aforementioned Charles Dillon (see footnote 98).

102   Probably based on Shakespeare's Queen Mab, described by Mercutio in *Romeo and Juliet*, 1.4, as a magical being who deals in dreams, enchanting people at night while they sleep ('She is the fairies' midwife, and she comes/In shape no bigger than an agate stone/On the forefinger of an alderman,/Drawn with a team of little atomies,/Over men's noses as they lie asleep').

believed he had got a bargain; he thought he knew what was the matter with him, and being a bit of a horse leech, thought he could cure him. By doctoring a little he managed to get him on his legs and into the street, and then he dropped down dead. The experience of horse buying cured me of any further speculation in horseflesh. I sold my stud, let my house, and went to Edinburgh, took to the Adelphi, but it proved a failure.

Pablo took the theatre off my hands, and, in company with my scene painter, Mr. Fitzgerald, I started off to find a place to build a theatre. Amongst other places, we visited York. It was the race week, and we had a narrow escape of being lodged in the lock-up at the police-station. Being the race week, as I have said, the police were on the look out for sharpers and the swell mob, so they bounced upon us (what blind men these policemen must be not to see the difference between professional buskins and light-fingered flash men). I say they pounced upon us, and would have dragged us to prison, in spite of *habeus corpus*,[103] if I had not bethought me of my luggage, and respectfully begged of the policeman that he would either let me look after my portmanteau or that he would be kind enough to see that it was properly taken care of, or it might be – so I suggested to him – that he would likely be held responsible for it, a risk which the policeman possibly thought we were not worth running for. So, on examining our luggage, he discovered that he had made a slight mistake, and we were thereupon set at liberty. I remained at York to see the races, but sent off Fitzgerald to Great Grimsby. He was to look for a place on which to build a theatre, and send me word when he had succeeded. Several days had elapsed without any tidings from him. I began to feel uneasy. I had furnished him with pocket money and a silver watch, to give him something like a gentlemanly appearance. One or two little things just then occurred to my mind, which, of themselves, would have been of little account, but, combined with this long silence, produced not a little scepticism respecting my friend's moral principle, so I determined to follow in pursuit, and not a moment too soon. When I reached Hull, I called at a theatrical public-house to see some friends belonging to the theatre, and heard by way of *on dit*[104] that a person was flashing

---

103   A writ ordering a person to be brought before a court or judge, so that the court may ascertain whether his/her detention is lawful. Here *habeas* is misspelt as *habeus* by Teasdale.

104   'rumour'; 'gossip'.

about Grimsby in search of a place suitable for a theatre, and that he seemed very flush of money, which he was very freely spending. I soon discovered, on enquiry, that it was my Man Friday.[105]

On reaching Grimsby, for which I lost no time, I found Fitzgerald as drunk as a lord. True, he had found a place, and a pretty place it was, as unsuitable for the object as if he had selected the top of the lighthouse; it would certainly have been more prominent, though hardly more inaccessible. When Fitzgerald was sober, I expressed to him pretty plainly the depth to which he had fallen in my esteem by his strange conduct. My next step was to substitute a more likely spot than the one Fitz. had selected for my new theatre. I took one near the market place, put it into the hands of the builder, and in eight days it was finished and opened with a tolerable company. I commenced with the monkey piece, which, as it was not the first time I had played it here, drew a very large audience and crowded the place, and this, too, notwithstanding the wet weather which flooded the theatre in some places ankle deep, and, at one period, reached the gas meter and put out the lights. The audience, nothing daunted, patiently waited until the water could be drained and the lights restored, and so the performance proceeded to the end. I remained here nine months, and received many marks of kindness from the fishermen, who presented me with more fish than we could eat. My success was so great that I was enabled to build a new theatre at the cost of £600, but, like the gambler's last stake, luck changed, and the tide – to borrow a simile from the locality of the scene – ebbed as rapidly, or more so, than it had flowed. Fitzgerald and one of the actors having quarrelled and fought in the street, I lost my licence, and was thus compelled to sell the place at a great sacrifice, having in vain attempted to keep it open as a concert hall.

I went to Burlington and opened the Corn Market as a theatre, and had a very excellent company. Alfred Raynor was the leading actor. It was my misfortune to have to take prisoner one of the guardians of the law, who had grossly insulted my wife and daughters. This compelled me to give him such a lesson of physical morality, that I have no doubt the law would ever after have a more faithful representative and guardian in the person of this erring officer. When the visitors began to come to this

---

105 A term for an efficient male aide or employee, derived from the character in Daniel Defoe's *Robinson Crusoe* (1719).

favourite watering place, we removed our theatre to the sea-side. There was a painter's shop which we converted into a theatre, but, which with all our manoeuvring, was much too small, especially as it was destined to be patronised and visited by no less a personage than a duke. Kean Buchanan, the American tragedian, was our leading "star."[106]

My next place was Bradford, where I was a great favourite, and was always treated at my benefit with a plumper.[107] One night, whilst performing the monkey, as I was running round the edge of the boxes, a gentleman, who ought to have known better, placed my life in great jeopardy by taking hold of my tail, and, but for my presence of mind in making a spring, which brought me on to the stage, I should certainly have been seriously injured. It was about this time that I made the acquaintance of three genial spirits, with whom I formed a close and intimate friendship. They were Americans, giving illustrations of Negro life, which they did with a grace and spirit which made them exceedingly attractive to the general public. Two of them were great drinkers, they spent all they got; the other was more temperate, and so saved money. I became greatly attached to them, and since I cannot forget old friends, my prayer for them is that the same grace which has changed my heart and character may make them the subjects of its triumphal power, and then shall we all be able to sing on a grander stage than the most royal theatre ever saw —

> *Oh! happy day that fixed my choice*
> *On Thee, my Saviour and my God*
> *Well may this glowing heart rejoice,*
> *And tell its raptures all abroad.*[108]

The following Christmas I went to Liverpool to play the clown at the Adelphi, but owing to some misunderstanding with the manager, I refused to perform. My successes had made me a little touchy; I was not the

---

106   Teasdale is probably referring to M'Kean Buchanan (1823-1872), a Shakespearean actor. Information taken from James Fisher's *Historical Dictionary of American Theater: Beginnings* (Maryland: Rowman & Littlefield, 2015), p. 86.

107 A word used to denote a crowd, or mass of people. It is sometimes used as a verb, to collect together. Teasdale is probably stating that his benefit drew a large audience.

108 'O Happy Day that Fixed my Choice', *Weslyan Sacred Harp*, c.1854. Originally by Philip Doddridge (1702-1751), published posthumously in 1755.

old Harvey of former days, but the Herr Teasdale of acknowledged fame. I at once telegraphed to Bradford to say that I was open to an engagement. Mr. Moseley immediately telegraphed back that I was to come at once, which, as I found that he had already engaged a clown, I accepted both as a compliment and a favour. I was as before, well received, and at the end of the season returned to Sheffield, and again took a public-house called the "Three Tuns."

I was next engaged by Mr. Coleman, of the Theatre Royal, to play the monkey in the Christmas burlesque of "Lord Bateman."[109] God has blest me with a constitution like iron, or it could not have endured the strain to which my wild and intemperate habits have subjected it. Many a time I have dressed myself for the night, performed the monkey, come back to the "Three Tuns," played at cards till the next night's performance without changing my dress, and again performed without any visible lack of energy, spirit, or vigour, the audience testifying by the same applause their appreciation of its merits.

The Easter following, Egerton, the Liverpool manager, came to Sheffield, and opened the Adelphi with a very splendid pantomime, got up in a first-class style. I was engaged as clown at a very advanced salary, which more than made up for the former difference between us. One night, whilst at the Adelphi, the militia, who had been called out on account of the Russian War,[110] were kicking up a great disturbance, going from house to house (public) smashing windows, glasses, and furniture, and beating every unhappy wight that came across their path. As I went I saw every public-house was closed but mine, and that, like an hospital, filled with bruised and maimed victims. Whilst my wife was relating what had taken place, the rioters returned, and I, with my usual impulsiveness and reckless indifference to consequences, rushed in amongst them, got struck across the face, nearly lost the use of one eye, and got my head laid open. At length a whole posse of police arrived, were severely

---

109   Folk song or play that tells the story of a Lord imprisoned in Turkey, rescued by a young woman, whom he marries seven years later. The specific play Teasdale refers to is probably *Lord Bateman: A Very Pretty Play in Three Acts* (1848).

110   The Crimean War (1853-1856) was a military conflict fought predominantly between the Ottoman Empire, Britain, France, and Sardinia against Russia.

handled, but ultimately succeeded in dispersing the rioters. The next day I had to go to the barracks to identify the delinquents, but, having had notice of my approach, the principal offenders made their escape from the barracks, were pursued, and two of them captured. One of them, Jack Robinson, had concealed himself on a rafter in a stable, and would have got clear off, but, having cut himself in the struggle, the blood dropped from the wound on to the policeman, which caused him to look up, and so he was taken. When before the magistrates, Mr. Dunn appealed to me for sympathy for them, on the ground that as they were going to fight the Russians I must not be hard upon them, which considering how much I was cut up by them, I thought was straining the quality of mercy too far; and so told Mr. Dunn that they might fight the Russians to their heart's content, but I should not allow them to practice on me for nothing.

I again left the public-house and took to theatrical management; opened the Huddersfield Theatre with an excellent company, and brought down the first-class "stars" of the profession – Mr. and Mrs. Charles Kean, Charles Mathews, Dillon, Kean Buchanan, John Coleman, Amy Sedgwick, Mude, and the Italian Opera Troupe.[111] Success followed – financially at least, but, alas, that was my ruin. Prosperity to me was a bane,

---

111   Mr Charles Kean (1811-1868) was the son of the aforementioned Edmund Kean, also an actor; Mrs Charles Kean (1805-1880), was known publicly as Ellen Tree until her marriage to Charles Kean in 1842, after which she went by her husband's name and performed with him on stage. Charles James Mathews (1803-1878) was an actor and theatre manager. He performed all over the world, producing over one hundred performances at Covent Garden alone. According to the *Hudson Collection of Early Sheffield Playbills*, Charles Dillon (1819-1881) 'gained widespread attention for his role of Hamlet at the City Theatre in London, he began to tour across the country's theatres. In this time, he took management posts at Wolverhampton, Sheffield and Drury Lane, London. He left England to tour the world with his wife, Clara in 1860, continuing to act up until his death' (p. 179). Kean Buchanan – see footnote 106. Teasdale probably refers to John Coleman (1831-1904), an apprentice architect before turning to acting, after which he performed and managed theatres in Sheffield, Leeds, and London. Amy Sedgwick (1830-1897) was a British actress famed for her comic performances, including Beatrice in Shakespeare's *Much Ado About Nothing*. The name Mr Mude repeatedly appears in playbills for performances at Sheffield theatres in the mid-nineteenth century. The *Hudson Collection of Early Sheffield Playbills* tells us that Mude 'rejuvenated Barnsley Theatre in his later years and regularly appeared on stage with the big names of his era, including … Mr Kean' (p. 184).

it only ministered to my vices and evil habits, and thus sowed the seeds of that misery and wretchedness which were to culminate in a prison, and might, but for God's interposing providence, have landed me on the gallows, or ended my career in the suicide's grave and the murderer's hell.

CHAPTER VI

It was about this time that there commenced those family and domestic troubles which, with indescribable horrors, all but unsettled my reason, drove me partially mad, and closed the dark side of my life with that midnight gloom which precedes the dawn of a bright existence, to be spent in the service of my Saviour and my God. Delicacy forbids that I should state the precise nature of those family troubles that maddened my brain, planted the thorns of jealousy – rankling like the fires of hell – in my bosom, and turned all the springs of life into wormwood and gall.[112] In a sudden fit of jealousy, with palpable grounds for its exercise, I broke up my home, sold my Huddersfield theatrical properties, rambled through the country, and became a heart-broken man. I had been serving the devil and he was paying me my wages. Like an unsettled spirit seeking rest, I wandered through the country with a troupe of serenaders, but I had no heart for the business, and tried to drown my troubles in drink; but there is no cure for a mind diseased – it only made matters worse. The only relief I experienced, and that only of a very partial character, was in the busy activities of life. I took an engagement to play clown at Dublin, and tried to forget my troubles by ministering to the mirth of the public. But what a mockery! How little does the motley, mirth-seeking audience of the theatre know of the bitterness of spirit that is hidden under the grinning mask and grotesque antics of the miserable clown who excites their thoughtless laughter.

While in Dublin, my wife, without any warning, left home, taking with her our two daughters, and leaving no traces of their flight. I searched Dublin through. This was on a Sunday afternoon. I had come

---

112   An idiom denoting strong feelings of resentment and bitterness. Gall is bile, a substance secreted from the liver and known for its bitterness; wormwood is a plant with a bitter taste. The expression originated in reference to various passages in the Bible, such as Lamentations 3:19 ('Remembering mine affliction and my misery, the wormwood and the gall').

home, expecting that tea would be ready for me as usual. The discovery of my wife's flight almost drove me mad. My search which was continued for several days, was ineffectual. After performing on Monday night with a feeling so hopeless and despairing that it was next to a miracle that I went through the performance without some fatal mishap, I cared not what became of me; death would have been hailed by me then as a deliverer from the greatest hell that could be realized on earth: so I told the manager that I could not perform again, that I would sail to England in search of my wife and daughters, whither I believed they had gone. Imagining that it was possible that they might have gone to Belfast to some music hall, I went there first, going from singing-room to singing-room, but all in vain. I then took my passage in a steamer to Fleetwood. The passage was an exceedingly rough one. Anyone who has travelled by those Irish packets, in which pigs and cattle are more cared for than the comfort of the passengers, may easily imagine what our condition was during that miserable voyage. The storm was so great that the pigs and people were hustled together; the cabin was filled with water, and the pigs were swimming, screaming, and struggling for very life. The storm increased to such a pitch that the vessel became a mere wreck, and when within fourteen miles of Fleetwood, signals of distress were fired, but it was some time before a steamer would venture out to us. At length we reached the harbour, amidst the shouts and congratulations of the crowd that lined the docks to welcome and rejoice in our safe deliverance from a watery grave.

I arrived at Sheffield, and found that my wife and daughters had not yet made their appearance; but, meeting with the agent of Mr. Pitt, of the Theatre Royal, I was induced, though with great reluctance, to take a night's engagement at the Royal as the monkey in "Jack Robinson,"[113] which drew a full house, and I obtained £6 for the night's performance. During the day my wife's sister received a letter, from which we learnt that my wife and daughters were still in Dublin. No inducement could therefore prevail upon me to give another night at the Royal. At the close of the performance I started by the mail train for Manchester, got a few hours' repose there, then took the mail train to Chester, and arrived in Dublin on Monday morning, found my wife and daughters, and brought

---

113   According to the *Hudson Collection of Early Sheffield Playbills,* Teasdale performed in 'Jack Robinson and His Monkey!' on 31st October 1850.

them back to Sheffield, with the exception of my eldest daughter, who refused to accompany us. I applied to the magistrates to interfere, but found that I had no control, she being of age, and thus mistress of her own actions.

I am compelled to allude to these family difficulties, though very reluctantly, because the great event of my life – my conversion to God – is so closely connected with their terrible consequences. The devil was now hurrying me on to what (unless gifted with the power of omniscience) he must have been assured was the doom of a murderer and a suicide. I am no theologian, nor is it necessary that I should be, in order to see that nothing but the direct interference of Divine power could save me from the necessary consequences of my own terribly impious and profanely wicked career. I do not profess to understand the mystery of God's decrees; I leave the higher doctrines of election and predestination to those whose learning, analytical and logical powers enable them to deal with such abstruse subjects. But of this I am assured, that I owe it to God's infinite love in Christ Jesus to poor sinners that I am now out of hell, and, blessed be His holy name, I am now in the way to the celestial kingdom. Nor is it less manifest to me that not only has Divine Providence interfered in a most marvellous manner on my behalf, but that Divine Grace has also performed a most surprising change in my inner man, so that I can not only say that "whereas I was blind, I now see,"[114] but that "being dead in trespasses and sins, I have now a new life within, working in me to will and do God's good pleasure."[115]

My evil genius again led me into the public-house business. I took one in Silver Street Head, called No. 3 Hotel; but whatever prosperity attended me in these places it always seemed a slow process of getting money: and with all its maddening scenes of drunkenness, idleness, and vice, it did not meet the requirements of my intensely active spirit that, for either good or evil, was ever hurrying me on. Enterprise, love of adventure, a craving for novelty and fame, were the leading qualities of my nature, and thus I never settled long in one place. I left No. 3 Hotel, engaged a troupe of serenaders, had a run through the country, lost what little money I had, and was only relieved by another monkey engagement

---

114   John 9:25 ('whereas I was blind, now I see').

115   Interpretation of Ephesians 2:5 ('Even when we were dead in sins, hath quickened us together with Christ').

at Manchester.

Again my domestic troubles were renewed. My wife again left me. I was tempted to commit suicide; and I remember when seeking my wife from town to town, I knelt down in one of the public streets in Stockport, and, in my wicked frenzy, prayed to the devil to relieve me of my misery. But the devil knows no pity for his victims. Being himself the victim of despair, his own aim is to make others as miserable as himself. My cup of wickedness being now full, I must reap what I had sown. "They that sow to the wind shall reap the whirlwind."[116] I had given my family the heritage of a wicked example. I had surrounded them with influences whose pollution angelic natures alone could withstand. That they should have succumbed was to be expected; I alone was to blame. The outraged laws of God and society have been partially avenged in the horrors, misery, and suffering which I have endured. I shall now very briefly relate the circumstances (which delicacy forbids me but to reca-pitulate) which brought me to Wakefield prison. My wife having again left me, and refusing to return, in my jealousy, and maddened by excite-ment, want of rest and food, I bought a pistol, got some drink, again sought my wife, and urged her to live with me again. She refused. I fired the pistol, happily missed my aim, and then tried to take my own life. With the razor in my hand, I was seized and taken to the lock-up, and, after examination before the magistrates, was committed to Wakefield to take my trial at the sessions.[117]

Thus ends the dark side of my life, but not my life itself. It might have been closed with the last dying speech and confession of a malefactor, a murderer, with the halter round his neck, a felon's grave within the precincts of the prison, and probably honoured with a niche in Madame Tussaud's dark gallery of celebrated criminals. That it has not thus ended is not to be attributed to any compunction on my part – no stopping short of the final catastrophe. The consummation was there; the act it-self was conceived and done; the consequences alone were averted by the direct interference of a merciful God who "willeth not the death of a sinner, but rather that he should repent and live."[118] The night I was

116   Hosea 8:7 ('For they have sown the wind, and they shall reap the whirlwind').

117 The sittings, or a sitting, of justice in court.

118   An interpretation of Ezekiel 33:11 ('I have no pleasure in the death of the

in the lock-up, after an abortive attempt on the life of my wife and that of my own, the whole of my past life, in vivid, panoramic succession, was presented before my mind's eye. Oh, the horrors of that night! The pressure was so strong, the strong heart was melted, contrition took the place of remorse, and it might have been uttered by the recording angel, "Behold, he prayeth."[119] It was probably the faint cry of an infant of grace struggling in the throes of a new and spiritual existence. I wanted to give my heart to God, but knew not how. Like many another newly awakened sinner, I wanted to purchase mercy by the promise of a new and holier life.

For many months I thus tried to obtain salvation by trying to roll the stone of Sisyphus up the hill.[120] But when God begins a good work in the sinner's soul, He never stops until He has finished it, and made that soul a temple for Himself. After my committal to Wakefield prison, in the receiving room I was asked what religion I was of. My reply was that I had none, but that I meant to have, and asked if I could have a Methodist minister to see me. I was informed that I must get leave from the visiting magistrates, which I accordingly did, and one was sent. I think his name was Waddy. It was not, however, through his instrumentality that I obtained pardon and peace. "God moves in a mysterious way His wonders to perform."[121] I had yet to be taught that "it is not by works of righteousness"[122] that the sinner enters the spiritual kingdom. I had tried hard, however, to get in that way.

Disappointment at last produced feelings of despair, sceptical doubts, and fears of having sinned beyond redemption. Satan now kept thundering in my ear, "Too late – too late!".

---

wicked; but that the wicked turn from his way and live: turn ye, turn ye from your evil ways').

119   Acts 9:11.

120   In Greek mythology, Sisyphus was doomed to push a boulder up a hill, only to have it roll back down again. He would repeat this task for eternity. Teasdale references the myth to express the initial fruitlessness of his struggle.

121 William Cowper, 'Light Shining Out of Darkness' (1772), published as part of the *Olney Hymns.*

122 Titus: 3:5 ('Not by works of righteousness which we have done, but according to his mercy he saved us').

THE LIGHT SIDE

CHAPTER VII

My work in the prison was at first to pick oakum,[123] but after my trial I was sent to make mats. Three days a week we went to chapel, in the morning; but in these devotional exercises I got but little comfort. I wanted pardon and peace, but the prison chapel exercises could not, or at least, did not, break through the distress and conviction of sin with which my soul was troubled.

One night in the month of July, 1864 – I shall never forget it – I had been struggling in prayer. The burden of sin – a sense of guilt and condemnation was pressing heavily on my spirit, the cry of my heart was – "I cannot let Thee go except Thou bless me."[124] To the eye of my faith was presented a sight of the Cross. My Saviour was there – the Lamb of God taking away sin by the sacrifice of Himself. At once the burden was gone. God, for Christ's sake, had pardoned my sin. All the night long I was praising God, and my fellow prisoners heard me. They, no doubt, thought that I was mad, and complained of my disturbing them. But that did not stop me; my joy was too great to be restrained by even prison discipline. Like, Mary, the mother of our Lord, "my soul did magnify the Lord, and my spirit rejoiced in God my Saviour."[125] Sleeping or waking it was the same. The visions of my bed partook of the same joyful theme. Three of these dreams, from their remarkable appropriateness to

---

123 Oakum picking was a common task given to those who were confined to prison or the workhouse and could not perform hard manual labour. A tedious process, it involved the unravelling of old rope to collect the oakum, a loose fibre often used for caulking seems in wooden ships.

124 Genesis 32:26 ('I will not let thee go, except thou bless me').

125 Luke 1:46-7 ('And Mary said, My soul doth magnify the Lord, And my spirit hath rejoiced in God my Saviour').

my condition, I may be permitted to relate. I thought I lived in a cottage, in the front of which was a garden. In coming through this garden to get to the cottage the ground began to sink, and I was being gradually swallowed up as in a quicksand. I cried to the Lord in my dream, and He rescued me from my impending doom. The lesson that I derived from this dream was – 1st, That no power on earth could save me from the inevitable consequences of that life of sin which had all but engulfed me in eternal ruin. 2nd, That I owed my deliverance to the direct interference and exercise of Almighty grace. The next dream was of similar import. I was passing through a narrow dark passage, at the end of which was a river, from whose gurgling waters I was snatched as by a miracle from a watery grave, from which I awoke only to realise the blessed consciousness of my deliverance, and to bless my Saviour who gave His own life to save mine. In the next dream there was a splendid vessel, in which I was sailing on the bosom of transparent waters in sight of the harbour, which we gallantly entered during the most glorious sunset I ever beheld. Was not this emblematical of the glorious consummation of Christian life in sight of the heavenly country which is to be his portion for ever? "Let me die the death of the righteous, and let my last end be like His."[126] After God had blessed me with the joy of His salvation, how rapidly the time seemed to pass.

> *What blissful hours I then enjoyed:*
> *How sweet their memory still.*[127]

Yes, there was joy in that felon's cell. Without egotism or presumption, I may say that angels then rejoiced over this brand plucked from the burning – this sinner plucked from the very jaws of hell. The gaol chaplain and schoolmaster asked me what I should do for a living when I left prison. Certainly the prospect of my return to society was not a promising one by any means. My monkey abilities were for ever buried in the pit of vice and misery from which I had been rescued. My conversion had closed the door of the stage to me for ever. I was like the lady I

---

126   Numbers 23:10.

127   Teasdale is probably referring to William Cowper, 'Walking With God' (1767), published as part of the *Olney Hymns* ('What peacefull Hours I then enjoy'd,/How sweet their Mem'ry still!').

heard of, who belonged to the Bowery Theatre in New York.[128] She had been induced to go to a Methodist Prayer Meeting. She went, and there the Lord met with her, convinced and converted her. She said to her new friends, whom she had met at the prayer meeting, "What must I do? I cannot go on to the stage again; but I am under an engagement at the theatre, and I have asked the manager to let me off, but he will not without my sacrificing all the money they owe me, and that will make a beggar of me." One gentleman said, "Madam, yours is a trying case; if I were in your place I'll tell you what I would do: I would spend the whole of the night in prayer for God to help me." She did so. She looked out of her window the next morning; she could see the theatre at a distance, but how surprised she was to see the theatre burnt down to the ground. Thus God released her from her engagement, and they were obliged to give her what was due. I could not go to the stage again, and as to the future supply of my temporal wants, it never troubled me. I felt conscious that He who had so wonderfully saved my precious soul would not fail to take care of my poor body. One thing I promised God; that I would never drink intoxicating drinks again, and, by His help I never will. When first I entered the prison, I wanted God to pardon my sins, and then take me to heaven; but when He had pardoned me, I wanted to live, to tell others "what great things the Lord had done for me."[129] I was not long, however before I learnt that one part of the heritage of God's people here is, that "through much tribulation they must enter the kingdom of heaven."[130] There was persecution even in Wakefield prison, of which I experienced no inconsiderable share. But what mattered it to me then? I felt that

> *I could smile at Satan's rage,*
> *And face a frowning world.*[131]

At length the day of my deliverance from prison came – November

---

128 The Bowery Theatre was situated on the Lower East Side of Manhattan, New York City. It burned down four times in seventeen years, with a fire in 1929 destroying it for good.

129   Psalms 126:3 ('The Lord hath done great things for us; whereof we are glad').

130 Acts 14:22 ('we must through much tribulation enter into the kingdom of God').

131   Isaac Watts, 'When I can Read my Title Clear', (1707).

9th, 1864 – but what a change had been effected since my entrance there! It was truly marvellous. I had been put into God's lavatory, and under its refining process what a transformation had taken place! I, the miserable slave of sin and Satan, had become an emancipated child of God. And now a new existence had opened before me. I was henceforth to serve a different master and to wear a new uniform; to fight against my old master, the devil, under the leadership of the Captain of the Lord's hosts, the Lord Jesus Christ. On leaving the prison, I was presented by the deputy-Governor with 2s. 6d. to make a fresh start in life with; but, with my new faith in Divine Providence, I felt no fear. The joy of the Lord made me strong. I could now say what I never could before —

> *Not fearing nor doubting with Christ on my side,*
> *I hope to die shouting, the Lord will provide.*[132]

Not long after my leaving prison, my former master, the devil had prepared a temptation for me. I received an offer of £7 per week to play the clown in the coming pantomime. It was whispered to me, "Resuscitate your finances by accepting this offer, and then quit the stage for ever." But He who had pardoned my sins gave me grace to resist the temptation and I refused the offer. When I reached Sheffield, I essayed to join the disciples of Christ, but, as in Paul's case, they did not believe I was a disciple. It was about this time the Hallelujah Band[133] was making so much noise, and being full of fire and zeal, I joined them. The marvellous changes which the grace of God had made in the character of some of these men called me to them as being myself a marvellous subject of the same wondrous grace. I signed the total abstinence pledge, gave myself up to the Lord's work, and spent the happiest Christmas that I had experienced for the last forty years.

The first Sunday in the New Year we went to Huddersfield to hold

---

132 An interpretation of John Newton's hymn 'The Lord Will Provide' (1779), published as part of the *Olney Hymns* ('No fearing or doubting,/With Christ on our side,/We hope to die shouting,/The Lord will provide').

133 William Booth (1829-1912), who would go on to establish the Salvation Army in 1878, formed the Hallelujah Band as a faction of the Revivalist Reform Movement of the nineteenth century. A motley crew of converted sinners, the Hallelujah Band were enlisted to help convert others.

revival services. We found the infidels[134] had a Sunday School to train up children in the rejection of God's truth – to teach them to despise the Bible, the only source of true morality and religion. When has Infidelity made a bad man a good one, a better father, a better husband? I have known it make good men bad men, but never the contrary. Yet Infidelity sometimes boasts of its triumphs and victories. Ignoble triumphs! worthy of being inscribed on the dark escutcheon of infamy, and the tablets of crime. So Satan may be supposed to rejoice amid the weeping and wailing, and gnashing of teeth. But, whatever success it has gained with the living, it has miserably failed with the dying. When the priest of Infidelity has stood by the bed of the dying – say, for instance, the hoary debauchee – and says to the worn out victim of lust and debauchery, "Fear not, old man, those spectres of the past, those ghosts of guilty pleasures long since forgotten, but now recalled by memory – busy, meddling memory – to haunt thy dying hours; they shall soon cease to annoy thee; there's peace in the grave, and no judgment beyond."[135] The old man shakes his head, the quivering lip and distorted countenance seem to say, "That doctrine may suit the bloom of health, but it won't wipe away the cold sweat of death; it soothes no more." No, Infidelity may do to live by, but it won't do, as an Infidel once said, to go over the falls of Niagara with. I never was an Infidel in theory, though God knows I've been one in practice. My mother's instructions in early life kept me from that. Many a time when I have taken those daring leaps, have I inwardly asked God to preserve me, and, as in the case of wicked King Ahab,[136] He has heard and answered me, for the prayer of the wicked is not always an abomination to Him.

I had in possession my clown and monkey dresses, with other stage properties. It was arranged between the members of the Band and myself that these should be publicly destroyed. So I took the Temperance Hall,[137] in Sheffield, which is computed to hold near 3,000 persons;

---

134 Literally meaning 'unfaithful'; infidel is a term sometimes used by religious groups to describe a person with no religious beliefs.

135 Teasdale is referring again here to *The Grave* by Robert Blair (see footnote 44).

136 According to 1 Kings 16:30, King Ahab was the wicked king of Israel, who, following the ways of his cruel wife, Jezebel, 'did evil in the sight of the Lord above all that were before him.'

137 The Temperance Movement advocated total abstinence from alcoholic

it was full, and many were unable to obtain admittance. The monkey dresses, &c., were burnt upon the stage. It was a blessed time; sixteen persons professed to find peace in believing – one, an old man, about sixty years of age. So may Satan's kingdom fall, and Christ increase His blood-washed throne!

I then took a tour through the country, giving my life's experience; God greatly blessed me, and through the relation of his marvellous mercy to me, the chief of sinners, hundreds have been brought into the same blessed state of peace and pardon. In Chesterfield I had four nights – crowded meetings – and more than eighty persons professed to have found the Saviour. The two first nights were in the Primitive Methodist Chapel. Cries of mercy were heard from all parts of the chapel, and no attempt was made to check these audible cries, which in most other chapels would have shocked the nerves of orderly Christians; but there the value of a soul is more thought of than the proprieties of mere conventional Christianity. Besides, what could be expected from prize-fighters, infidels, poor fallen women, backsliders, and sinners of the lowest grade? And these were the characters who, knowing my former life, were drawn together to hear my experience. Surely, they thought, if he has found mercy, why may not we? And He who had mercy on a Magdalen was there, not to rebuke their noise, but to change the cry for mercy into songs of praise. There was one poor woman who seemed greatly distressed; she had a beautiful child in her arms. I spoke to her about giving her heart to Christ; she shook her head, and I could get no word from her. I felt interested in the woman, and I stayed some time talking to her, pleading earnestly with her for present decision; but the only reply to my pleading was a shake of the head. I was compelled to say to her that I was afraid that her love for her child prevented her giving her heart to her Saviour, and that if it was so, God might see it necessary to take away the child to save her soul. This seemed to strike home, for with a shudder she pressed the unconscious infant to her bosom, as if to say, "No, not my child; I cannot part with my child." I left her, and it was weeks before I saw her again, but I may as well here relate the sequel. Whilst attending the market at Chesterfield, I was accosted by a woman, who asked me if I did not remember her. I said I had not the slightest recollection of her.

beverages. As a movement it grew during the nineteenth century, and by 1835 the British Association for the Promotion of Temperance was established.

She recalled to my memory the circumstance of the woman and child in the Primitive Methodist Chapel, and what I had said to her. I then remembered her, and I noticed also that she was dressed in deep mourning, as for a near relative. She told me with a sob of anguish such as only a mother can express, that God had indeed taken away her child – robbed her of her child, but that she was more than comforted by realising His pardoning mercy and forgiving love.

From Chesterfield I went to Mansfield, and, though but a few hours' notice was given, the Primitive Methodist Chapel was crowded, and sixteen souls were brought into the fold. One, a poor young man who had but just come out of prison, hearing that I had been in one, was struck with conviction, and, like another inhabitant of a prison cried out, "What must I do to be saved?" and then, believing in Christ, he also rejoiced. In Mansfield, I commenced attending the market with a stall of cutlery, &c., but it did not do much for me, or I might have taken up my abode there. From Mansfield I went to Clay Cross, and had a good time, feeling greatly the presence of the Spirit in my own soul. Some time after I again visited Chesterfield, and found that the devil had been busy in trying to undo the work which had been begun. The report had got about – how, no one could tell – that I had returned to my theatrical pursuits, in fact, a kind of ubiquity was given to my performance, for I was reported to be "starring" and playing the clown in three places at once. My return to Chesterfield was therefore hailed by many with joy, as a contradiction and rebuke to the malicious slander that had been so industriously circulated against me. As a set off to the annoying attempts of my enemies to injure me, it was now that I met with the woman whose child God had taken to save her soul. I did indeed rejoice at that poor woman's conversion. The painful dispensation by which it was effected is full of instruction, as showing the variety of means, the inexhaustible armoury, from which God draws his shafts to reach the hearts of sinners, and to baffle and destroy the dominion of the devil. "The Lord whom ye seek shall suddenly come to His temple, but who may abide the day of His coming; for he shall be like a refiner's fire, and like fuller's soap."[138]

---

138 An abbreviation of Malachi 3:1-2 ('the Lord, whom ye seek, shall suddenly come to his temple, even the messenger of the covenant, whom ye delight in: behold, he shall come, saith the Lord of hosts. But who may abide the day of his coming? and who shall stand when he appeareth? for he is like a refiner's fire,

I have quoted the above passage because it will illustrate much of what I am now about to record of my own experience. It is well for us poor weak mortals that the veil which hides the future from our gaze, and which so many foolishly wish to penetrate, can only be gradually unclosed. If the drops that compose the dose be so bitter and unpalatable, what must the full cup be. "Sufficient for the day is the evil thereof."[139]

It was now reported of me that I was trying the "pious dodge," – that I was endeavouring to make money by preaching. This touched me in a sensitive part, for if there is one failing to which I am more subjected than another, it is the pride of independence. It shall never be said of me, with truth, that I am either too proud or too lazy to work for my living. The imputation of hypocrisy and covetousness grieved me. To give the lie to the base insinuation, I determined to go to some village, and, entering upon the lowest calling, work my way up to position and influence. Accordingly I went to a village called Totley, near Dore, in Derbyshire, and took a hut near the Moor, with a large piece of ground for a garden, for which I paid 1s. 3d. per week. I bought a small stock of smallwares,[140] travelled about the country with a hamper fixed on two wheels, to hold my merchandise, which I sold or exchanged for rags and bones. Often have I travelled sixteen miles a day, dragging a heavy load over very rough roads, sometimes ready to fall through fatigue and weakness. For nine weeks I lived on bread and tea – no sugar, no butter, no butchers' meat ever passed my lips the whole of that time. But what did it matter to me; I was engaged in my Master's work, scattering the seed of Divine Truth among the villages through which I passed and occasionally giving addresses in chapels or schoolrooms when I had the opportunity to do so. It was a little wounding to my pride, I must confess, when crying "rags and bones,"[141] to have to submit to the jeers and ridicule with which the ignorant and rude would assail my humble calling. A strange contrast it seemed to those who had known me in former days, rolling in wealth in the devil's service. Some freak of fortune or deserved judgment was, no

and like fullers' soap').

139 Matthew 6:34 ('Sufficient unto the day is the evil thereof').

140 Small articles of merchandise.

141 Often living in extreme poverty, the rag and bone man would typically collect small items to sell on to merchants. He would sometimes have a cart to carry his wares.

doubt, to conclusion drawn; but I was happier – far happier – then, even with poverty and persecutions (for I had both) – than ever I had been in the possession of wealth and sin. It was, however, no monkish asceticism that induced me to accept this low calling; I felt that I was in the way of Providence, and that He who had subjected me to the humiliation would, in his own time, lift me up from the vale of poverty, and I was willing to wait for the gracious interposition. Whilst I could say —

> O, poverty, where are thy charms,
> Which sages have seen in thy face?
> Better dwell in the midst of alarms,
> Than with poverty stand face to face.[142]

Yet, with greater feeling still, I could sing, with Dr. Watts —

> Father, I wait Thy daily will,
> Thou shalt divide my portion still,
> Grant me on earth what seems Thee best,
> Till death and heaven reveal the rest.[143]

One day I had been to Hathersage, and from thence to Hope, travelling 22 miles, and taking altogether between two and three shillings; and when crossing Dore, about two o'clock in the morning, one of the wheels of my trap broke.[144] Here was a pretty fix, in the midst of a wild, desolate moor, with no house nearer than my own humble domicile. Somebody says it is a necessity of life to meet with difficulties, but the glory of life to overcome them. I managed somehow to reach home in about two hours, and never was home, poor though it was, so welcome to me as that little hut at Totley. After thanking God for my safe landing, and all His mercies, I retired to my bed, which was a mattress, with a rug for my covering, and slept as sweet and sound as a monarch might upon

---

142   Teasdale's interpretation of William Cowper's 'Verses, Supposed to be Written by Alexander Selkirk, During His Solitary Abode in the Island of Juan Fernandez' (1782). Cowper's text reads as follows: 'Oh solitude! where are the charms/That sages have seen in thy face?/Better dwell in the midst of alarms,/Than reign in this horrible place.'

143   Isaac Watts, 'How vast the treasure we possess', *Hymns and Spiritual Songs* (c. 1709).

144   Hathersage and Hope are both towns in north-east Derbyshire.

his downy bed. After I had been at Totley four months, I bought a small hand-cart, with four wheels, to which I made a covered top like a gipsy's tent. But, as many a small tradesman has found before me, the supply of one want often creates another, so my new cart seemed to me to necessitate the possession of a donkey in order to draw it – an acquisition that was, however, easier thought of than obtained. At length the wished-for boon was realised. A donkey, whose name (for what is a donkey even, without a name?) was Charley, was purchased. This was a great advance in my trading operations, though, in truth, it was but a sorry investment. I never was a judge of animals, as the reader knows, and the donkey was no exception; I was told he was about two years old, but I found afterwards that he was nearer thirty. He had many bad faults, I knew, but I was told they were the follies of youth, to be corrected by age and proper treatment; but, alas! they were confirmed, ineradicable faults, which no kindness could conquer, and no severity expunge. Charley was, however, a great assistance in bringing my rags and bones to Sheffield to be disposed of. But Charley being country born and bred, and not used to city life, when he got to Sheffield became quite stupefied, and every now and then would sit down on his hind quarters, looking the very picture of bewilderment, and no coaxing or beating would make him move until the fit had passed. While the jeers of the crowds of passers-by were buzzing in my ears and goading my spirit, I could really envy the stolidity of the animal, who sat unmoved amidst it all. Charley's equanimity was truly wonderful.

I received a letter from Mr. Unwin, of the Sheffield Hallelujah Band, asking me to take part in some religious services which the band were about to hold at Oldham during the fair. Having accepted the invitation, I set off with Charley, the gipsy cart, and an increased stock of merchandise, intending to trade on the way. The distance was forty miles, eleven of which was dreary moorland, and it took us nearly three days to do it. The journey over the moor was under a pouring rain, which drenched me to the skin. It was exceedingly disagreeable to Charley, and no inducement could make him go more than a mile an hour. For seven hours the rain continued pouring down as from a bursting cloud. Not a shed could be seen to give even a partial resting place. To my dying day I shall never forget the discomfort and misery of that dreary journey; and never did the following hymn appear so sweet to me, as when singing it on that lonely moor —

> *Though often we are weary, there is sweet rest above –*
> *A rest that is eternal, where all is peace and love;*
> *O! let us then press forward, that glorious rest to gain,*
> *We'll soon be free from sorrow, from toil, and care and pain.*
> *There is sweet rest in heaven, &c.*

> *Come Christians, don't grow weary, but let us journey on;*
> *The moments will not tarry – this life will soon be gone;*
> *Our Captain's gone before us, He bid us all to come,*
> *High up in endless glory, to our eternal home.*

> *Loved ones have gone before us, they beckon us away,*
> *O'er heavenly plains they're soaring, blest in eternal day*
> *But we are in the army, and dare not leave our post.*
> *We'll fight until we conquer the foe's most mighty host.*

> *Our Saviour will be with us, e'en to our journey's end,*
> *In every sore affliction, His present help to lend;*
> *He never will grow weary, though often we request,*
> *He'll give us grace to conquer, and take us home to rest.*[145]

I have heard of a little sweep boy, who, whilst sweeping the chimney was heard singing, at the top of his voice —

> *The sorrows of the mind*
> *Be banished from this place;*
> *Religion never was designed*
> *To make our pleasure less.*[146]

And I have found that the hymns of Zion[147] are better calculated to sustain the spirit under its heaviest burdens, to give courage to the

---

145   Anonymous, 'Though often here we're weary', *Hymns for Social Worship* (1861).

146   Isaac Watts, *We're Marching to Zion* (c. 1707).

147   Teasdale is probably referring to lively, spirited hymns, similar to Watts's *We're Marching to Zion*. Zion is the hill on which the city of Jerusalem stands. Its earliest mention is in 2 Samuel 5:7 ('Nevertheless David took the strong hold of Zion: the same is the city of David').

fainting heart, and drive away the demon of despair, than the logic of the highest reason, or the inductions of the most profound philosophy. The army of Cromwell,[148] it is said, was never more invulnerable than when the soldiers went into under the inspiration, and whilst singing the Psalms of David.[149] My trading professions on the road were very inauspicious, taking little more than bought provisions for myself and donkey, and on one occasion, when near Oldham, we had to camp out on the road, the donkey grazing hard by the road side, and, myself attempting to sleep under the canopy of my gipsy tent, I was alarmed during the night by a whistle, apparently a signal, which was soon after followed by another. By and by the tent covering was lifted. Some marauder, tempted by my little store, I thought, was paying me a visit. But my fears were soon dispelled; the sudden beam of a bullseye revealed, not the law-breakers, but the peace-preservers, a couple of policemen, holloaing out, "what are you doing there?" to which I replied, "trying to sleep, but cannot." We reached Oldham on Saturday morning, opened my stall, and took 6d. during the day – not a very promising provision for Sunday's needs; but after I had packed up my goods for the night, a man came up who had known me as manager of the Oldham Theatre, and bought a lot of things, which enabled me to make a proper provision for the day of rest. A happy day it was. We held services in the public hall during the day, and on the following days on the fair ground, and many souls were saved. We started on Wednesday morning for the return journey, and without any great mishap reached home at last.

Being now pressed by my friends to come to Sheffield to reside, and feeling that my health was suffering from the severity of a bad winter, I was not sorry to leave a place which presented no prospect of either

---

148   Oliver Cromwell (1599-1658) was a puritan military and political leader who would serve as Lord Protector of the Commonwealth of England, Scotland, and Ireland from 1653 until his death.

149   Cromwell encouraged his army, often referred to as 'Ironsides', to sing psalms while going into battle. *The Soldiers' Pocket Bible* (c. 1643), containing several psalms, was distributed to Cromwell's soldiers for religious inspiration and to boost morale. According to Cromwell, through instilling the fear of God into his soldiers and rallying them together in prayer and song, they never lost a battle. Teasdale uses this example to demonstrate the strength and courage religion inspires when compared to the less motivational tenets of 'logic of the highest reason, or the inductions of the most profound philosophy'.

physical or spiritual improvement; so, having paid my rent, I packed up my things, which Charley, by a little extra coaxing in the matter of a few luxuries in the way of eating, brought safely to Sheffield. My wife having now returned to me, I became doubly solicitous for her conversion. My prayers, which were presented night and day on her behalf, were graciously answered. Having joined the Church, under the pastoral care of the Rev. R. Stainton, my wife, under his powerful ministry, became, through the operation of the Holy Ghost, awakened to a sense of her condition, and savingly converted to God; and now, glory be to His name, we can both worship at the same family altar, rejoice in the same Almighty Saviour, and anticipate the spending of a blessed eternity in His glorified kingdom. I may say here, and I do it with feelings of devout gratitude, that I feel myself under deep obligation to the Rev. R. Stainton for many acts of personal kindness which I have received from him, and also that my views of Christian truth have been greatly enlarged and developed under his ministry. May God long continue and increase those signal proofs of usefulness and spiritual prosperity which have so wonderfully accompanied his preaching.

I have now little to add, save that I have parted with Charley, the gipsy tent, and all my valuable store, for the large sum of 6s. 6d., and have embarked in a new business more congenial to my spirit, and, I trust, replete with opportunities of usefulness.

APPENDIX: TRANSCRIPTS OF NEWSPAPER ARTICLES

Sheffield & Rotherham Independent, 24th January, 1865

THE "MAN MONKEY" IN A NEW CHARACTER.—

From time to time during the last few months, the inhabitants of Sheffield have been startled with a series of sensational announcements, concerning the services of the Hallelujah Band, at the Temperance Hall. "Convicted felons, prize fighters, pigeon stealers, dog fighters, wife beaters, poachers, &c., &c.," have been announced to give "their experience," and the result of the extraordinary concentration of talent, or rather character, has been crowded houses. Last week, the walls were placarded with the announcement that last night "Harvey Teasdale," the converted clown, would publicly destroy his stage dresses, the manuscript plays and music, and his pantomime tricks and books. To meet the expenses connected with this "extraordinary engagement," charges were made for admission, but notwithstanding this, the hall was crowded to excess in every part. The gallery was filled with an audience strongly reminding one of the "gods" of a cheap theatre, while in the body were to be found very many who had seen Harvey Teasdale as the "Man Monkey," and were anxious to see his disposal of the character and its appurtenances. The business of the evening – it can hardly be called a service – commenced by a hymn sung with extraordinary gusto by the large audience, the refrain being the favourite part, and as such was subjected to frequent repetition. Prayer by a member of the band followed, and upon the Chairman announcing an address by another member, great uproar and cries of "Harvey" followed. After silence was procured, the address was given, but was listened to very impatiently. At its conclusion, Harvey Teasdale came to the front of the platform, and was greeted with loud cheers, and those peculiar whistles and calls which must have been familiar to him in his theatrical days. These, however, were stopped by one of the leaders announcing that that was a "religious service" – a fact which could hardly have been known unless it was stated. Teasdale came forward and produced a bag containing his "properties." He announced that Mr. Edward Lauri, clown at the Surrey Theatre, had kindly consented to be present and see that all were destroyed, and that the properties and books were real - and this statement appeared to be very satisfactory to the audience, who greeted Mr. Lauri with a hearty cheer. The work of demolition then commenced, Teasdale producing a dress which he said belonged to the "Dumb Man of Manchester," and handing it over to the brethren behind, who, with large shears and knives, quickly destroyed it. The dresses of "Scaramouch," and the other favourite characters of Teasdale, shared the same fate, while the motley garb of the clown, with the cap which "had gone through the clock face for the last time," were speedily reduced to shreds. The manuscript plays followed, each being handed to Mr. Lauri first for examination, and Teasdale explaining the various pieces and relating some anecdote connected with them. Mr. Lauri explained his presence that night, by stating that all the pieces had been offered to him for £2. 10s., but that they had been refused to him. He was in Leeds that afternoon, and there he heard that Teasdale had destroyed the same things there, and so he had come down to see. This statement created some laughter, ad provoked from Teasdale the remark that he had enemies in Leeds. The audience watched the destruction eagerly, hailing the names of the more prominent pieces with loud shouts, and Teasdale was frequently requested "to play it over again." When Mr. Lauri was examining some "original" music, said to be worth "£10 to any manager," he was urged to "pocket it," and frequently the same advice was tendered to him with no avail. The last property to be destroyed was "the monkey," and the audience were requested "not to be frightened," although it was "very hideous." A large stuffed figure was then brought on. It was the monkey dress of Teasdale stuffed with shavings "to give the people an idea of Harvey Teasdale as he was," and no sooner was it brought upon the platform than it was seized and literally dragged to pieces by the enthusiastic band, amid great uproar mingled with shouts of "Hallelujah." This concluded the principal part of the business, and a hymn was given out. The attempt to sing was, however, a failure, and it was abandoned at the end of the first verse. An address of an unusually florid and frantic style, from a converted prize fighter and nigger minstrel followed, after which the musical disposition of the audience was again tested, and this time with greater success. Various other addresses and hymns followed, and the proceedings, which were of the most extraordinary character and beggared description, were concluded about ten o'clock.

Sheffield & Rotherham Independent, 25th January, 1865.

THE HALLELUJAH BAND.

TO THE EDITOR. – I have just read with feelings of intense disgust, in your issue of to-day, a paragraph headed, "The Man Monkey in a new character." Surely, Sir, Sheffield is degenerating from its usual intellectual position when such blasphemous scenes as are now constantly enacted in the Temperance Hall are not only tolerated, but witnessed with evident complacency by crowds of apparently respectable people – scenes that, as your reporter says, beggar description: where the Trinity is addressed as an ordinary acquaintance, and alternately bullied and coaxed in a horribly irreverent and unseemly manner by convicted thieves, &c.; where prayers are but frantic howlings and the wildest gesticulations; where exhortations are unintelligible ravings; where hymns are ludicrous nigger melodies of the lowest and most unintellectual stamp, such as –

> "The devil and me, we cannot agree;
> I don't like him, and he doesn't like me;" &c.

Where impressionable young females are surrounded by gangs of shouting, dancing, yelling fanatics; frightened and bullied until they are on the point of fainting, and then dragged indecently to the front and called converted; where, in short, decency is outraged, religion burlesqued, and the Almighty mocked and insulted. It is incomprehensible how anyone with a grain of common sense can imagine that God is honoured by such means as these. Again: is it to be borne that a premium should thus be put upon villainy by honouring, promoting, ad supporting in idleness men who have justly forfeited all claim to the respect of their fellow creatures by their repeated crimes, merely because they have become or have pretended to become religious? A positive and direct inducement to felony is thus held out. You can become a thief, and when thieving ceases to pay undergo a pretended "conversion," and you at once become a religious celebrity, and gain an excellent living without the trouble of working for it; while if you remain honest, you may both profess and possess religion, and yet remain a nobody, and be compelled to earn your bread by the sweat of your brow. Surely, Sir, some means should be devised to put an end to these demoralising and disgusting spectres.

Yours,
ANTI-HUMBUG.
January 24th, 1865.

Sheffield & Rotherham Independent, 26th January, 1865

Three responses to Anti-Humbug's letter, the last of which argues that

> scores of poor degraded sinners are being elevated, raised from the deepest sinks of vice, immorality, and crime, and are becoming honest, sober, and industrious, through the humble instrumentality of the Hallelujah Band.

and that the Temperance Hall has swelled the ranks of Primitive Methodists, Free Church and Wesleyan Reformers.

Sheffield & Rotherham Independent, 28th January, 1865

TO THE EDITOR.—Your correspondent "Anti-Humbug," states in your paper of yesterday, that I am receiving from the Hallelujah Band 25s. per week for my services. I beg to assure him, and the public generally, that I do not receive one farthing from the above Band. I am more than paid for my services in the happiness of knowing that the Almighty has permitted me to be a humble instrument in his hands in assisting the above Band in winning souls to Him. If your correspondent will put me in the way of earning 20s. per week, in any honest business I am able to do, I shall be very thankful.—

Your humble servant,
Harvey Teasdale

Sheffield & Rotherham Independent, 28th January, 1865

THE HALLELUJAH BAND [...]

The circumstances were these: – when Harvey Teasdale determined to lead a Christian life, he knew that it was necessary to get rid of his dresses and manuscripts, as they would be both an incumbrance and a temptation. He therefore advertised them for sale in a London newspaper, on the 24th of December. Some of the Hallelujah Band advised him not to sell or give manuscripts or dresses, as they would again be used in the service of Satan [...] The newspaper with advertisement referred to was read by a person in the gallery, which raised a storm against Harvey Teasdale, but when he had given an explanation, which was most triumphant, he won the whole audience to his side [... As Teasdale] described in chaste and poetic language the scene on Calvary, the audience was hushed, the "roughs" appeared spell-bound; and I believe that every Christian man who heard it had one wish – that Harvey Teasdale might have the opportunity of giving that address to tens of thousands of his perishing countrymen.-

Yours truly,
VERITAS

Sheffield & Rotherham Independent, 30th January, 1865

Mr. Lauri writes in to confirm that music and MSS were there but says dresses were just 'old rags'.

Sheffield & Rotherham Independent, 2nd February, 1865

THE HALLELUJAH BAND

TO THE EDITOR.-- "Anti-Humbug" is anxious to know what became of the money taken at the Temperance Hall on the occasion of my theatrical property being destroyed. This is a proof that he did not attend on that night, or he would have known that I announced from the platform that the overplus of money, after paying all expenses, would be given to help me until I got into some business whereby I could earn an honest living, which announcement was received with loud cheers, as your reporter can testify. Your correspondent further states that "destroying my theatrical property is an old trick of mine (oh malicious dame!); that it has been done in Leeds and elsewhere." I declare before my God that never such a thought ever entered into my mind until advised by my Sheffield friends to do so on the above occasion. I defy "Anti-Humbug," or anyone else to prove my having done so before that evening. Your correspondent wants to know if the seven pounds per week offered me was only for the Christmas pantomime. Decidedly, only for that time. But let him not for a moment think that I should have been idle for the rest of the year. I have received six pounds per night for my representation of the monkey at the Theatre Royal, Sheffield, and in various parts of the country have received as much as twenty pounds per night for my services in the above character. But, bless the Lord, Harvey Teasdale is transformed from a sensation clown and man-monkey to a child of God! Let me advise "Anti-Humbug" to pay more attention to his Bible, if he has got one; if not, let him wait upon me, and I shall be only too happy to supply him. Let him get more charity in his heart, and less ill-will to those whose only aim is to do good in trying to bring poor misguided sinners from misery and wretchedness to seek that true happiness which can only be obtained through the atoning blood of our blessed Redeemer. – Thanking you for inserting my two former letters, I remain, your very humble servant,

HARVEY TEASDALE

Bramwell Street, St. Philip's Road, Feb. 1st.

P.S.- I do not intend to answer any more newspaper letters; my time can be used to a better purpose. I ought to have stated in the above letter that that the only towns I have visited since out of prison have been Huddersfield, Rotherham, and Barnsley - a Sunday in each town for religious purposes.

Sheffield & Rotherham Independent, 5th August, 1862

ATTEMPTED MURDER AND SUICIDE AT SHEFFIELD.

An attempt at murder and self-destruction transpired in Sheffield yesterday afternoon. The principal actor is Harvey Teasdale, comedian, and the intended victim is his wife. The parties reside in Blind lane, and for some time past appear to have been living unhappily together, mutual recriminations respecting each other's conjugal fidelity being of frequent occurrence. The neighbours say that both were faulty, and that each contributed their quota to the cause of domestic bickerings and strife. A little before four o'clock yesterday afternoon Teasdale went to his house, in company with a man. On arriving on the steps of the house, it is said, he turned suddenly round and struck his companion a blow in the face with his fist, which sent him rolling into the street. He then rushed into the house, fastened the door on the inside, and directly afterwards the report of a pistol was heard. This alarmed the neighbours and passers by, and a rush was made by several persons towards the door and the windows of the dwelling, which resisted their efforts to force for a few moments. Happily they soon gave way, and the house was entered by various persons, among whom was Mr. Linley, tobacconist, Bow street. The wife was discovered with her face covered with blood, and Teasdale with his head lying back on the sofa, in the act of drawing a razor across his own throat. He was immediately seized, and prevented from carrying out his suicidal design. The police were quickly on the spot, and as the prisoner had only inflicted a slight gash on the throat, he was at once conveyed to the Town Hall on a cab. The unfortunate woman's face was sadly disfigured, especially on the right side, but the pistol could only have contained powder, or she must have been killed instantaneously. She was removed to the Sheffield Infirmary, where she now lies, and we believe there is every hope of her ultimate recovery. It is said that the prisoner stated that only yesterday morning he had gone down on his knees to his wife and begged her to give up her present course of life and leave the neighbourhood in which she was living, and that she replied that all she wanted was to be away from him. This he assigns act with which he now stands charged [sic.]. He also said that he had been obliged to give up four theatrical engagements lately through her conduct, and that she was training up her two girls to be as bad as herself. The act was evidently a premeditated one if the above statement be correct. The prisoner will be brought up at the Town Hall today.

Sheffield & Rotherham Independent, 12th December, 1862

YORKSHIRE WINTER GAOL DELIVERY…THE CHARGE AGAINST HARVEY TEASDALE.

The Grand Jury returned true bills against Harvey Teasdale on two indictments – one for shooting with intent to maim, and the other for feloniously wounding. Mr. V. BLACKBURN, who was for the prosecution, applied to his Lordship for permission to send up a bill to the Grand Jury for an attempt to murder. His Lordship refused to interfere.

Sheffield & Rotherham Independent, 13th December, 1862

THE CHARGE AGAINST HARVEY TEASDALE

HARVEY TEASDALE, 46, indicted for feloniously wounding his wife, Sarah Teasdale, at Sheffield the 4th August last. Mr VERNON BLACKBURN prosecuted, and Mr . SHAW defended the prisoner. Mr. Blackburn, in stating the case, said he could not go into the charge which had been preferred against the prisoner of shooting at his wife with a pistol, but would go upon the charge of wounding with a razor, with intent to do grievous bodily harm. If he proved the facts which he was instructed to open to the Jury, he could not see how they could do otherwise than find the prisoner guilty of the felony; although, if they saw any reason, they might reduce the offence to that of unlawfully wounding, which was only a misdemeanour. The prisoner had alleged that his wife had been unfaithful to him, but that was unsupported by any evidence. The witnesses were called:—

Sarah Teasdale, wife of the prisoner, said: The prisoner is a comedian. In July last we went to St Helen's in Jersey. I left him with his consent early in July, and he paid my fare to Manchester. I went from Manchester to Sheffield, to the house of a person named Hewitt in Holly street, a friend of mine. On Saturday, the 2nd of August, I saw the prisoner in Sheffield. He came to Mr. Hewitt's shop, and saw me, and asked me to go back with him. He said, will you come and live with me; and I told him he had treated me so badly I would not go back. He stayed there about six hours. On the following Monday I saw him about three o'clock. I was sitting in the front-room, facing the door. The prisoner came to the door, which was open. He said, "Come here;" and I said, "If you want me come here." He pushed a young man off the step, came into the room, locked the door, and then immediately turned round and fired a pistol at me. I was hit upon the face, and was stunned for a minute or two. When I came round I saw him opening a razor. He came up to me as I lay on the floor, and cut my throat with the razor. He cut me more than once on the throat, and also on the cheek and hands. The window was then opened, and young Mr. Hewitt, who had been on the doorstep before, came in and took the prisoner off me. I had not said anything to the prisoner as to what he would do to himself.

By Mr. Shaw: We had been married about twenty-six years. He was a spring-knife cutter before he became a comedian. I had been seven days at Sheffield before he came to me. He was in great distress, and wished me very much to go back and live with him. He did not get on his knees and ask me to go back with him.

Henry Hewitt said: I am a sheep-shear maker, residing with my mother in Holly street, Sheffield. On the 4th of August, at half-past three, the prisoner came up to me as I was standing at the door of the house. He closed the door behind me, which pushed me off the step. He locked the door after him. Directly afterwards, I heard him say to his wife, "Are you coming across?" There was no reply that I heard. Directly afterwards, I heard the report of the pistol. I went to the window and saw the prisoner kneeling by his wife, cutting her throat with a razor. I sprang through the window and took him off her, and took him to the Town Hall. Mrs Teasdale was in a fainting condition on the floor. There was blood upon her.

Mr. Marriot Hall, assistant house-surgeon at the Infirmary, said: On the 4th of August, Mrs Teasdale was brought to the Infirmary. She had a wound 2½ inches long on the throat, and a large discolouration on the face. She had also some slight cuts on the face. There was some bleeding, but she had not lost very much blood. The discolouration was produced by powder; the wound on the throat by some sharp implement. She was in the house eleven days, and under my care afterwards three weeks. The wound was not dangerous, but it was in a very dangerous place.

Detective-officer Winn produced the razor which the prisoner had used.

THE PRISONER'S STATEMENT BEFORE THE BENCH AT SHEFFIELD

"Four months ago we were staying in Leeds. I have been married to her 26 years. I loved the ground she walked on, and she hated me. While we were at Leeds she left her home one Saturday morning. I went in search of her, and for the first time I found that she was getting her living on the streets, and she boasted that I had not found her out. She had always men waiting of her, and I traced her from Leeds to Huddersfield. She was in a low locality. I came to Sheffield fair. She came to me; we got together. I was at Sheffield three weeks. Eventually we went to St. Helen's. We had not been there many days before she left me. I chased her to Manchester; from there to Stockport, and ten to Ashton; still living this unfortunate life. From there she went to Huddersfield, and then to Manchester with her daughter and three gentlemen. Eventually they told me she had started for Sheffield. This was last Saturday fortnight. I took the first train and came to Sheffield. I went direct to Blind lane. I sat with her for six hours, endeavouring to persuade her to leave this course of life. She said she would stand at the window and see me cut my throat, and would not let my corpse come into the house. I told her she would drive me mad, and it would end in suicide. She said she would like to see it. I went to a public-house across the street to a friend of hers; I got her to go across. I stayed there till after nine o'clock at night. I went across myself to Mrs. Hewitt's to buy a pie. It is a pie shop. I begged my wife to come out. She said I was a fool to follow her. I went home. I felt I could not live without her, On the Monday morning I went to my wife again. She would not go with me. I left her and wandered about. It caused me to get a little drink, and having had nothing to eat, and part of my skull taken out, I made up my mind to commit suicide, and to go to her house to do it. I called at a public-house, and called for a glass of ale, and then it was that I put the powder into the pistol; but I only did it to frighten her. I never intended to hurt her. I did not intend to fire at her at all. I bought the razor two or three minutes before. I gave threepence for it. I remember nothing after I entered the house. The pistol must have gone off whilst we were scuffling. We use pistols on the stage. My intention was to frighten her, and cut my own throat."

Mr. Shaw, in addressing the Jury, said the facts of the case against the prisoner were incontestable, and he would not abuse the patience of the Jury by arguing against them. It was a most lamentable case. The prisoner when he committed the act was in great distress of mind, caused by his wife's refusal to live with him. The only question for the Jury to consider was, with what intent did the prisoner use the razor. They must see that if he had intended to kill his wife he would have struck the razor upon her throat with greater force, and have thereby inflicted, if not a fatal, at least a more dangerous, wound. There was no pretence for saying that the pistol which he fired was loaded with anything more dangerous than powder; and the learned Council contended that the only object of the prisoner was to alarm his wife and frighten her into going back to live with him. That being the case, the Jury would be justified in finding the prisoner guilty of unlawfully wounding only.

His Lordship, in summing up, said: It was not an unreasonable thing to assume that a man meant to that which was the consequence of the act that he did. In this case the wound in itself was not dangerous, but it had been inflicted in a very dangerous region. The Jury might, if they could see any reason for doing so, find the prisoner guilty of the minor offence, but at the same time they might be satisfied that he did not intend to do his wife any grievous bodily harm.... The Jury, to the surprise of the whole court, found the prisoner guilty of unlawfully wounding..... His Lordship said the Jury had taken a very merciful view of the case. Probably they had considered, from the state of the prisoner's mind at the time, that he had not formed any definite intent which would warrant them in convicting him of the felony. If they had convicted the prisoner of the felony, he would most undoubtedly have been sentenced to a very long period of penal servitude. The offence of which he had been convicted was one of the most aggravated character, and he (the Judge) felt it would be his duty to sentence him to the longest term of imprisonment the law allowed, which was that he be kept to hard labour in the gaol for two years.

Printed in Great Britain
by Amazon